SCROLL SAW FRETWORK

Techniques & Projects

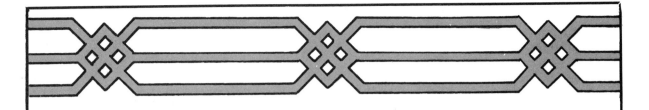

SCROLL SAW
FRETWORK
Techniques & Projects

Patrick Spielman &
James Reidle

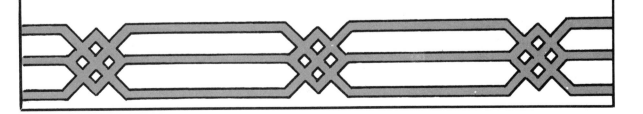

Sterling Publishing Co., Inc.   New York

Edited by Michael Cea

Library of Congress Cataloging-in-Publication Data

Spielman, Patrick E.
    Scroll saw fretwork techniques & projects / Patrick Spielman and
James Reidle.
        p. cm.
    Includes index.
    ISBN 0-8069-6874-5
    1. Fretwork.   2. Jig saws.   I. Reidle, James.   II. Title.
III. Title: Scroll saw fretwork techniques and projects.
TT186.S669   1989
745.51—dc20   89-35458
                                                                        CIP

Copyright © 1990 by Patrick Spielman and James Reidle
Published by Sterling Publishing Co., Inc.
387 Park Avenue South, New York, N.Y. 10016
Distributed in Canada by Sterling Publishing
c/o Canadian Manda Group, P.O. Box 920, Station U
Toronto, Ontario, Canada M8Z 5P9
Distributed in Great Britain and Europe by Cassell PLC
Artillery House, Artillery Row, London SW1P 1RT, England
Distributed in Australia by Capricorn Ltd.
P.O. Box 665, Lane Cove, NSW 2066
Manufactured in the United States of America
All rights reserved

CONTENTS

ACKNOWLEDGMENTS

We are very grateful to the many individuals who shared their vast experiences, expert knowledge, and various resources with us.

First and foremost, we extend our appreciation and our heartiest thanks to Henry Aldinger for his valuable assistance in so many areas. Henry afforded us the use of his rare, old, and delicate reference sources. He helped us trace the history of scroll saws and fretwork, provided a number of excellent photographs, and was kind enough to review our chapter on fretwork and scroll-saw history.

Another key source of information was Gus Stefureac, from Raleigh, North Carolina. Gus is the premier expert on old foot-powered tools in the United States; we appreciate his significant assistance in this research and his loan of valuable resource material from his extensive collections.

We also express our gratitude to Carl Weckhorst, our good friend and probably the most productive fretworker ever, and to his lovely wife Phyllis. They allowed us to convert their home into a studio as we photographed Carl's outstanding fretwork pieces.

Kirk Ratajesak, also known as the Fretworker, has given us terrific insight into the world of scroll-sawed fretwork miniatures, which he creates and sells professionally. Thank you, Kirk, for sharing your techniques and plans, which will be most valuable for our readers regardless of the size of their fretwork projects.

John Polhemus of J. P. Woodworks, Waldorf, Maryland, provided many fretwork projects for us to photograph that illustrate some excellent scroll-sawing techniques. We are most grateful to John for generously allowing us to include many of his unique designs and ideas, which are sure to motivate and inspire all those who touch a scroll saw.

The late Lawrence Boehner, who cut all his fretwork with a hand-held fretsaw, allowed us to include some examples of his work, and shared his expertise on how to use the hand saw. His work illustrates the fantastic projects that one can make with only a few tools.

Another key individual in this collaborative effort is our artist and colleague, Dirk Boelman, of The Art Factory, Richland Center, Wisconsin. His valuable and versatile talents often extended well beyond his spectacular pen and ink work, which we are very pleased to offer our readers.

Other individuals, companies, and crafts people who helped us in a variety of ways include: Ray Seymore of the Seyco Sales Co.; Hanns Derke of Advanced Machinery Imports, Ltd.; Ray Lawler of The Tool Company; Scott Phillips of Shopsmith Inc.; Zach Etheridge of Highland Hardware; Tom Martin of Sakura, U.S.A.; Don Thomas of Procyon Machine Tools; Gene Sliga of Delta International Machinery Corp.; Jerry Cohen of the Lancaster Machinery Co.; Don Strong and Guy Shore of Strong Tool Design; Ron Barlow of Windmill Publishing Co.; and the Cumberland Woodcraft Co., Inc.

Thanks also to the following: expert craftsman Ro Jodat for his sawing tips; historian

Michael Knight for his notes; and craftsmen Conrad Jensen and Ken Gould for their assistance. We thank Mark Obernberger for his special drawings, and offer thanks once again to Julie Kiehnau, our tireless, efficient typist.

And finally, but certainly not least of all, we express our gratitude and love to our spouses, Elaine Reidle and Patricia Spielman, and to our children, who always were helpful and especially supportive in every way every day.

Patrick Spielman,
Spielmans Wood Works, and
James Reidle,
Reidle Products

INTRODUCTION

Essentially, fretwork is considered fine scroll-saw work and excludes traditional marquetry and inlaying techniques. Sometimes, fretwork is more simply described as sawing away the background of a pattern. (See Illus. 1.) This type of fretwork primarily, but not exclusively, involves sawing pieces with many inside openings to create ornamental or grill-like objects. (See Illus. 2.) Through fretwork, you can make exceptional decorative and practical products for the home or office.

Illus. 1. *This ornate thermometer plaque made by Carl Weckhorst is a typical example of traditional fretwork.*

Illus. 2. *This fretwork clock, made by Carl Weckhorst, involved a combination of sawing and assembly techniques that included piercing, the use of contrasting overlays, and fine joinery in the mitre assemblies of the thin material.*

Illus. 3. The constant-tension saws, introduced in the 1970s, can be used to make delicate and ornate fret cuts in 2 inch and thicker material.

Almost all early fretwork was cut with hand frames or foot-powered saws. The wood material used in the home shop to making fret-cut objects was not normally more than ½ inch thick, with most of it closer to ¼ inch. Since the introduction of the constant-tension saws in the late 1970s (Illus. 3), many new avenues for creative and artistic scroll saw work have been created. Now the scroll sawer can make very precise and delicate fret cuts in thick wood material (Illus. 4), as well as in traditional thin-wood materials. One new saw can make clean and accurate cuts that are perfectly vertical in soft woods 2¾ inches thick! Another new saw kit is designed especially for sawing thin fretwork and operates at an optimum speed for such work that is about ⅓ the speed of most other machines.

Technically, machines labeled jigsaws and sabre saws can also be used to cut fret objects, but they are usually limited in these applications. The term jigsaw pertains to those machines with rigid overarms. These saws have a narrow blade that vertically moves against the tension provided by a spring located directly above the blade. Sabre saws are regarded as hand-held devices or machines that reciprocate much stiffer and larger-sized blades that are only clamped on one end. Sabre saws are not used for fine or delicate fretwork.

Fretwork was extremely popular in the

Illus. 4. A fretted shelf bracket cut from stock ¾ inch thick.

United States and Europe from the mid-1800s to the 1940s. It was a productive hobby for men and women of any age or economic background. Today, there seems to be a growing resurgence in the popularity of fretwork in particular and in scroll sawing in general. There are many reasons for this. First, fretwork today, like the fretwork of the past, can be done by anyone with a modest income. Also, it is the ideal hobby for those interested in getting started in handicrafts. Anyone who uses a scroll saw will quickly find himself making objects that are useful and decorative. (See Illus. 5.) And scroll saws are the least hazardous of all power tools.

Fretwork seems to add a richer dimension to wood, and thus provides a good medium for those artistically inclined. It is also recommended as a way to utilize the seemingly never-ending energy of youngsters, who may find themselves devoting more and more of their leisure time to fretwork. And it provides hours of productive diversion for senior citizens who are active.

There are other advantages to fretwork. It can be started and discontinued at will. It only makes a slight mess, which can be cleaned up quickly. And you can easily and inexpensively obtain the tools and materials needed to start. Even the most economical of

tools can produce good results. In fact, it's possible to start with nothing more than a hand frame and an inexpensive drill, and your kitchen table as a work area. Soon, however, you will progress to a scroll saw, but even in this situation you will only need a minimum of work space and a few additional tools and supplies.

Thinner woods are still used in the majority of fretwork, so you can start with one of the lower-priced scroll saws, which cut thin wood well. If you want to cut thicker frets, you will have to buy one of the more expensive machines. In the following pages, you will learn how to produce more and better-quality work with the less-expensive scroll saws and how to get the most from the higher-priced machines.

No matter which scroll- or fret-cutting machine you decide to use, be very careful when selecting one. Consider the different saw features in terms of how they will satisfy your own sawing needs. Two vital considerations are how quickly and conveniently the blade can be threaded and changed, and whether the saw can accurately cut thin or

Illus. 5. A fretwork chess/checker board is a fun, useful, and unique project to make with your scroll saw.

thick materials (as you choose) in hard or soft woods at the speed you prefer with minimum blade breakage or any other problems. This book explores these factors, and many more.

Chapter I charts the essential historical development of fretwork and the evolution of the modern scroll saw. Further chapters center around the new tools, machines, and accessories available on the market.

Also examined are the basic techniques for using the new, thin plywood and easy-to-apply finishes that make fretwork easier and more fun. With these techniques, you can produce high quality work more quickly.

A chapter on special techniques details among other methods ways to make and apply fretted overlays and to cut fretted letters and signs. Included are ideas for veining leaves and employing simple-sawn line work to artistically enhance silhouettes. (See Illus.

6.) Also explored are ways to combine fret sawing with simple carving techniques to create some intriguing projects.

Chapter VII, which deals with the joints and their assembly, offers additional useful techniques and jigs. For example, the improved "shooting board" detailed will allow you to make extremely accurate mitres and an array of bevel cuts with only a hand plane.

A number of full-size fretwork project patterns are also included. These patterns are a selected sampling from our companion book, *Scroll Saw Fretwork Patterns*, and have been chosen to provide some good starting projects for beginners and to challenge the experienced scroll sawer. Both the black-and-white photos that appear throughout the book and the full-color photos shown in the color section illustrate some phenomenal fretwork projects that were made by several scroll-sawing experts.

Illus. 6. An example of fret-sawn lettering and the use of veining, a technique in which saw cut lines are used to give more "life" and interest to silhouettes and similar projects.

I
HISTORY OF FRETWORK AND SCROLL SAWING

Fretwork is the sawing of very ornate and decorative items with numerous inside or cutout openings and designs that involve an array of quick sharp turns. It is a form of craftwork that was very popular in the past and is just now being rediscovered. (See Illus. 7.)

This form of light woodworking was in fact extremely popular in the United States from the mid-1800s through the 1930s. It was also very popular in England and Germany. At that time, everyone made fretwork projects, including women and schoolage boys and girls. Even though, as we will see later, the tools used then may today seem crude, the skill or output by those who did fretwork was not diminished.

Though making fretwork pieces was generally considered a recreational pastime, in some circles it was considered a serious art form and, in others, a viable business activity. Fancy Victorian scroll work was in demand because it was so popular in architecture. Wooden household accessories and gingerbread embellishments embodied sawn ornamental designs of fretwork that had a lot of delicate detailing.

The fretwork made in the home shop was primarily cut from solid wood stock, usually ¼ inch and less in thickness. Larger saws were used in factories to cut the heavier, thick brackets and sawn architectural ornaments that were so popular in the 19th century.

Tools were generally inexpensive. As is the case now, a wide assortment of different sawing devices were available, ranging from a very inexpensive hand-held frame to relatively sophisticated foot-powered scroll-sawing machines with functioning parts that looked and worked much like some modern constant-tension scroll saws.

It's really very difficult to determine exactly where and when in history fretwork had its very first beginnings. Egyptian furniture removed from sealed tombs provides proof that veneers were used as ornamental fret-like overlays some 3,000 years ago. And delicately cut veneers also appeared on early Greek and Roman furniture. Ornamental overlays on furniture were also found in European and Scandinavian countries in the 16th and 17th centuries.

Elaborate fret furniture parts were clearly evident in the works by the famous 18th-century European craftsmen, including Duncan Phyfe, Thomas Chippendale (1740–1780), and others. Some of Chippendale's fret designs were inspired by the repetitious geometrical patterns found in early Chinese temples.

Basic fretwork techniques and recognizable special tools can clearly be traced back to a famous French craftsman, Andre Charles Boulle of Paris (1642–1732). His expertise actually involved the decoration of furniture with brass tortoise shells and exotic wood inlays. Boulle is regarded by some historians as

It was even called a "bracket saw" because shelf brackets were a popular project cut with it. Eventually, it was called the fret saw, a name that has survived up to today. It remains virtually unchanged in its basic design.

Fretwork became very popular in Italy during the mid-1700s, where it was actually called Sorrento Carving because most of the famous fretworkers practiced their art in the city of Sorrento. The term Sorrento Carving spread throughout the world and became the label for fretwork, even in the United States. (See Illus. 11.)

The Sorrento Wood Carving Company of Boston and Chicago was founded in 1865,

Illus. 7. This fretwork clock is one of many made by James Reidle, Sr. on an early foot-powered scroll saw. This project stands an impressive 50 inches high. More photos of it and other projects are shown in Chapter IX.

the father of inlay and marquetry techniques. His ornamental work became so specialized and well known that eventually it was simply described as "Buhl-Work"—(Buhl was the German corruption of Boulle's name).

The U-shaped saw frame Boulle used was called the Buhl saw and various other names over the ensuing years. (See Illus. 8 and 9.)

Illus. 8. Buhl sawing around 1775. Note how the workpiece is clamped in a vertical position on the "donkey" or "Buhl horse." The cutting is done with a push stroke. Two jaws hold the work firmly with foot pressure. One hand manipulates the workpiece, in coordination with the foot clamp, while the other hand moves the saw horizontally.

Illus. 9. The Buhl saw was later called the bracket saw and, finally, the fret saw. This type of saw has remained virtually unchanged since the 1600s. It is still available today and is sometimes used by fret cutters and marketry experts. When using it, insert the blade so that the teeth point towards the handle and support the workpiece in a horizontal position. The technique is shown on page 98.

Illus. 10. In the early 1850s, elegant Spanish ladies enjoyed wearing these huge (up to 6 feet across) wooden fret-sawn "head pieces" (combs). Just consider the obvious problems these head pieces created when the ladies moved about in crowded streets, shops, or at the theater.

Illus. 11. Fretwork, also known earlier as Sorrento wood-carving, was a popular hobby for everyone including women and children from the 1800s through the 1940s and into the early 1950s.

and claimed to be the only mail-order house in the world devoted solely to fretwork. It provided all the necessary tools and featured German patterns and expensive high-quality saw blades made from clock spring steel. It also is quoted as claiming to be "The first to introduce this knowledge of this pleasing work into this country." (See Illus. 12 and 13.)

In an old catalogue, "Schroeter's Scroll Saw Designs, Revised Edition No. 1," dated 1915, the following is written on the inside cover: "Fret sawing of fancy articles originated in Switzerland using in all cases the old style hand frame. . . ." It further adds: "A Boston lady while traveling there conceived the idea of introducing this most fascinating work

into this country as a novel and useful mode of recreation. On her return she brought with her a number of these small frames with a quantity of fine blades and patterns. In connection with her other business, she introduced this charming work, and found it gave great satisfaction, and that the applicants for these outfits were so numerous that she had often to renew her stock from abroad. But the interest grew so rapidly that she commenced to the manufacture of frames (saws) in this country. Up to this time the cost of these outfits and instructions were quite an item, and naturally the wealthy alone could enjoy them. But an enterprising firm saw the necessity of placing an article of

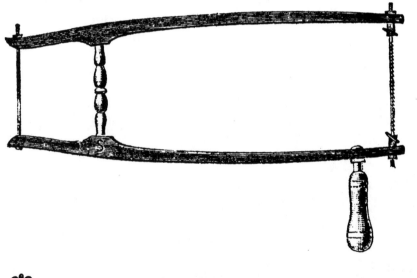

Illus. 12. Varying styles of wooden saw frames were made so that larger pieces of fretwork could be made. The design shown here was the popular choice of the ladies who operated the Sorrento Wood Carving Co. in Boston. When used, long frames such as this were supported on the upper arm to reduce fatigue.

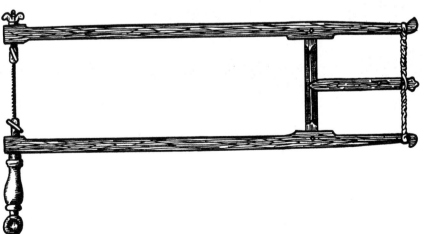

Illus. 13. Another version of the fret-saw frame.

this kind upon the market that would reach the masses and began the manufacture and introduction of their cheap outfit, which gave good satisfaction, and had wonderfully large sales, reaching into the hundreds of thousands."

This trend continued for several years and around 1867 crude foot-powered scroll saws for home use began to appear. In fact, during the last half of the 1800s close to 50 different models or variations of foot-powered scroll saws arrived on the market. (See Illus. 14.) Various tables and guides for hand-saw frames also appeared. (See Illus. 15.)

Prior to the foot-powered scroll saws that were made for home use, crude factory saws were already developed that operated according to the movable sash (wooden frame) principle. (See Illus. 16 and 17.) These saws incorporated some fundamental design principles that were retained in some of the saws made early in this century and even in today's modern saws.

Some of the medium-duty scroll saws made in the 1800s were lathe and scroll-saw combination units. A number are illustrated in this chapter. Then, as now, there were also homemade scroll saws that were either saw attachments made to fit on spinning-wheel frames or attachments used on foot-powered sewing-machine stands. The Our Family scroll saw, offered in an 1875 catalogue, was a commercially produced unit used in combination with a sewing-machine head.

There were at least 14 designers or printers of fretwork patterns in the 1800s. (See Illus. 19–22.) Many mail-order houses that sprung up at that time offered everything the fret sawer needed, including machines, blades, wood hardware equipment, and thousands of project patterns. Of the many project designers of that era, the most illustrious include Adams and Bishop. They founded their company in 1879 and later sold it to J. R. Bowman. "Russell's Designs of 1884–85" featured patterns by Arthur Hope and H. L. and William Wild. Other names involved with the creation and/or distribution of patterns include Fleetwood, Pomeroy, and Ware.

Patterns were also imported. Many of these patterns were of English, Dutch, Ital-

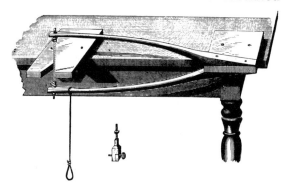

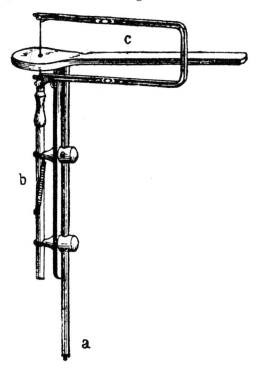

Illus. 14 (above). This ingenious device clearly employing foot power dates back to the 1860s or 1870s. For plans and illustrations of the author's version of this foot saw turn to pages 185–187. Illus. 15 (right). Fuller's patented attachment for use with the steel fret-saw frame ensured an accurate vertical saw motion. (a) An adjustable rod which is raised or lowered according to table height. Hand force is required to effect the downward motion of the saw, but a spring at "b" raises the frame back to position. The entire unit is secured to the table at "c." The adjustable leg is connected by a hinge to permit sawing at an angle.

Illus. 16 (above left). This reciprocation saw of 1775 with the bow-spring action above is the forerunner of the industrial jigsaws that were later driven by water-powered line shafts. Illus. 17 (above right). This very early version of a scroll saw, Talpey's scroll saw, was patented in 1865 by Jos. A Talpey. It employed a foot treadle that lowered the "sash" (saw frame), which consisted of the arms and the strained blade. The upper arm was attached to a wooden spring that immediately raised the sash (carrying the blade) after each downward stroke.

Illus. 18. Roy Underhill (left), master woodworker of PBS's television, examines Gus Stefureac's antique piece of elegant, European late-1800 fretwork that also incorporates some outstanding veneer inlay and marquetry work. Stefureac, from Raleigh, North Carolina, has one of the largest collections of old scroll saws in the country. It consists of foot-powered tools of all kinds, but primarily from the Post-Civil-War Era.

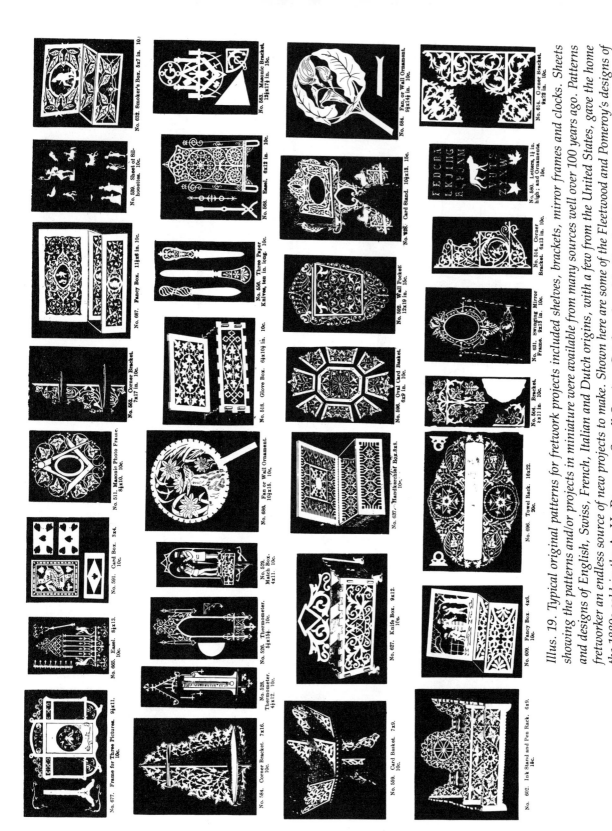

Illus. 19. Typical original patterns for fretwork projects included shelves, brackets, mirror frames and clocks. Sheets showing the patterns and/or projects in miniature were available from many sources well over 100 years ago. Patterns and designs of English, Swiss, French, Italian and Dutch origins, with a few from the United States, gave the home fretworker an endless source of new projects to make. Shown here are some of the Fleetwood and Pomeroy's designs of the 1880s sold in the A. H. Pomeroy Scroll Sawing Catalog, based in Hartford Connecticut.

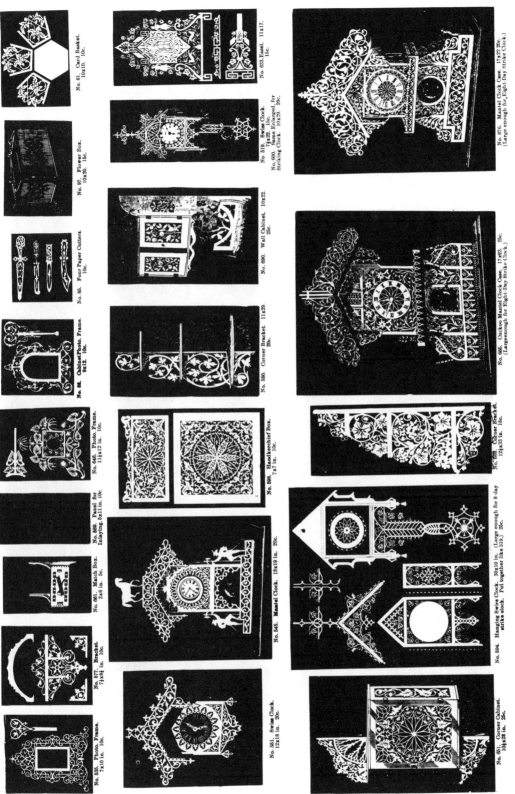

Illus. 20. Another one of the 22 catalog pages from the A. H. Pomeroy Scroll Sawing Catalog.

No. 22—Corner Bracket.
6x18.   Price 15 cts.

No. 158—Easel for Panel Picture.
Price 10 cts.

No. 189—Wall Cabinet.
6x13.   Price 15 cts.

No. 304—Mantel Shelf.
7x13.   Price 15 cts.

No. 192—Card Basket.
7x11.   Price 10 cts.

No. 191—Card Basket Swing.
7x10.   Price 15 cts.

No. 255—Three Shelf Bracket
15x21.   Price 20 cts.

No. 307—Casket.
11x12x16.   Price 20 cts.

No. 127—Book Shelves.
10x29.   Price 20 cts.

No. 126—Corner Bracket.
11x31.   Price 20 cts.

No. 125—Corner Bracket.
11x29.   Price 20 cts.

No. 308—Mantel Shelf or Window Cornice.
7x15.   Price 15 cts.

No. 309—Cabinet Frame.
7x10.   Price 10 cts.

No. 310—Two Match Receivers.
6x11.   Price 10 cts.

No. 311—Wall Bracket.
12x17.   Price 10 cts.

No. 264.—Toilet Mirror.
9x12.   Price 10 cts.

No. 306—Clock, enlarged from
No. 212.   13x25.   Price 25 cts.

Illus. 21. One of eight pages from the Russell's New Designs, *1884–85 catalog.*

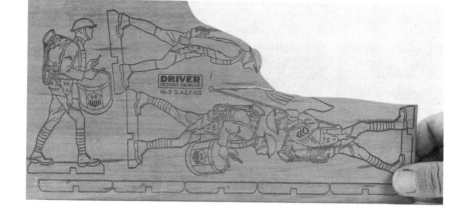

Illus. 22. Some of the early woodworking supply houses not only provided patterns, but also sold specially prepared thin woods for fret sawers. Some even provided patterns preprinted directly onto the wood, such as this example from the collection of Gus Stefureac.

DRIVER
DESIGNS ON WOOD
No. 5 D. A.E.F.103

20

ian, German and French origins. When the total quantity is considered, relatively few were Americans. There was also one magazine called the *Fret Sawer's Monthly and Home Decorator* which provided tips and introduced new patterns, tools, and supplies.

The actual development of foot-powered scroll saws intended for the amateur or home craftsman began in the 1870s. Once it began, many saws began to appear in rapid succession. In 1876, A. H. Shipman of Rochester, New York claimed to be the first to manufacture a cheap, practical foot-powered scroll saw for home use. Appropriately named the Centennial because of the year, Shipman's saw, though crude, was sold in the United States and abroad with great success. Within

Illus. 24. The early Companion scroll saw (1870s) still had many parts made of wood. Here it is shown with a lathe and drill attachment. The price for the saw & drill together was only $3.00.

three years, his workforce grew from 10 to over 200 employees. Up until this time the treadle on the foot-powered scroll saw produced a rotary motion; on the Shipman saw, this motion was converted to a vertical reciprocating sawing action. Other saw models produced and improved by Shipman's company included saws with names such as the Demas for 1880, Demas No's. 4 and 5 (Illus. 25), the Prize Demas (Illus. 26), the Holly, and the Prize Holly (Illus. 29).

The Millers Falls Co. of New York also produced some saws in the 1870s and 1880s that became very well known, and were used throughout this country and presumably abroad. The most popular were its Cricket and Rogers saws, which were very inexpensive and could be afforded by almost all home crafts people. (See Illus. 30–34.) Other saws produced by Millers Falls Co. include the Millers Falls Saw (Illus. 35), the Star, the

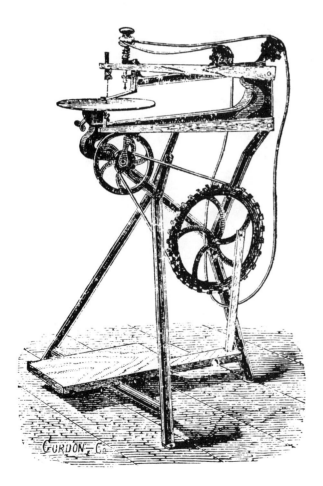

Illus. 23. This 1879 saw with many wooden parts was called the Iron Centennial.

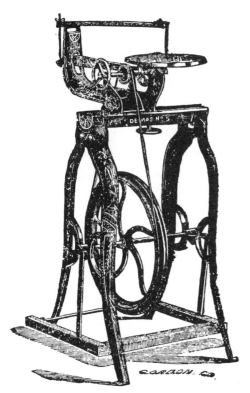

Illus. 25 (above left). The Demas No. 5 saw was designed for heavier work. It cut stock 2 inches thick and had a 24-inch throat capacity. Illus. 26 (above right). Shown here is the new Prize Demas Lathe and Scroll Saw Combination Machine. The scroll saw has a 1¾-inch cutting stroke, a 20-inch throat, and a lathe that can swing stock 5 inches in diameter by 16 inches in length.

Illus. 27. The Improved Demas (also called the No. 3 Demas) was manufactured in the 1880s by A. H. Shipman of Rochester, New York. This was one of the best combination lathe scroll saws available. Both tools could be run at the same time, or, the manufacturer claimed, the saw could be "thrown in or out of position in five seconds without removing any part of either machine."

Illus. 28 (above left). Here is another version of the Improved Demas, with the saw tipped out of position to facilitate lathe work. (Photo courtesy of Henry Aldinger) Illus. 29 (above right). This "Prize" Holly Scroll Saw was an improved model over earlier versions, probably the third in a line of saws manufactured and distributed by the A. H. Shipman Co., of Rochester, New York.

Illus. 30 (right). The Cricket Saw was developed to meet the demand for a cheap foot-powered saw. It had wooden arms, weighed only 17 pounds, had a throat capacity of 16½ inches, and cost only $2.50. It was recommended as a starter saw for small boys. The new Rogers Saw was very similar to the Cricket except it had a blower, drilling attachment, optional emery wheel, and sold for about $3.50. Illus. 31 (far right). This Rogers saw was among eight models manufactured by the Miller Falls Co. between the 1870s and early 1900s.

Illus. 32. The new Rogers saw (1880–1915) was perhaps the most popular of all the treadle saws. (Photo courtesy of Henry Aldinger)

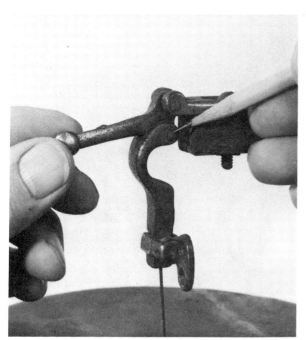

Illus. 33 (above left). The blade clamp on the new Rogers saw featured a toggle-type lever tensioning mechanism that operated two pivots on a linkage. Illus. 34 (above right). The blade clamp lever in its tensioned position.

Illus. 35. The Millers Falls Scroll Saw No. 387 dates back to somewhere between 1885 and 1895. (Photo courtesy of Henry Aldinger)

(Illus. 44), the Victor (Illus. 45 and 46), and the Empire.

The W. F. and John Barnes Co. of Rockford, Illinois was the major foot-powered scroll-saw manufacturer in the Midwest. Two brothers, one a model maker and the other an inventor, organized their company in 1868. Officially established in 1872, this company made a number of innovative and efficient foot-powered scroll saws and eventually branched into all kinds of woodworking machinery, including foot-powered lathes, shapers, table saws, and other tools. Its tools became extremely popular and its scroll-saw machines are now highly sought by tool collectors.

Some machines were made for light indus-

Lester (Illus. 37), and the New Lester (Illus. 38).

The Trump Bros. of Wilmington, Delaware started to introduce a number of saws in the 1870s. One of the company's earliest innovative saws was the Fleetwood, which had a friction drive. (See Illus. 36 and 39.) Later models (1879) were redesigned from friction to the more conventional belt drives. In addition to three different models of the Fleetwood saws, the Trump Bros. also made the Dexter saws—Models A, B, and C. (See Illus. 40 and 41.)

The Seneca Mfg. Co. of Seneca Falls, New York made at least six high-quality saws. They were given names such as the Challenge or Boss (Illus. 42 and 43), the Rival

Illus. 36. The Fleetwood, one of the Trump Bros.' earliest saws, had a friction drive.

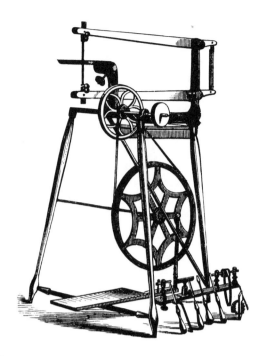

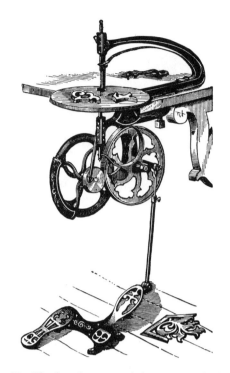

Illus. 37. The Lester Saw was manufactured by Millers Falls Co. of New York between 1870 and 1900. The Millers Falls Co. produced at least eight different machines.

Illus. 39. The bench-mounted foot-powered Fleetwood scroll saw, first patented in 1872, was claimed to be the best for delicate and accurate fret sawing. It had a first-class ornamental stand, unique guided saw blade clamps, a 14½-inch throat capacity and could cut stock 3–4 inches and under rapidly.

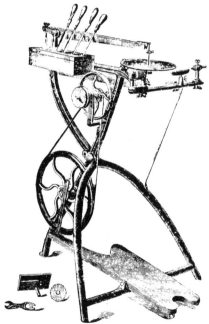

Illus. 38. The 1879 New Lester Saw had an 18-inch cutting capacity and clamps that held any size and length of blade and faced them in any one of four directions. It was also used as a lathe, a small circular saw, and had drilling and emery wheel attachments.

Illus. 40. The Dexter "A" was designed for table or bench top use.

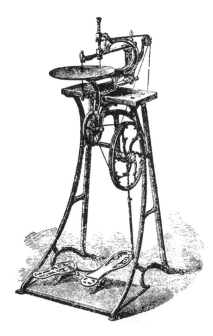

Illus. 41. This Mounted Dexter was one of three models that carried the Dexter name in the 1870s and 1880s.

Illus. 43. The Challenge scroll saw designed for steam power.

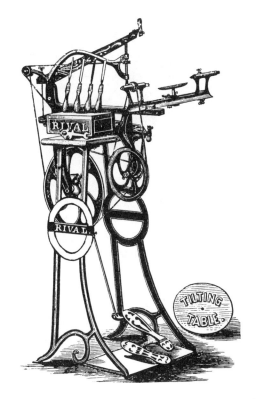

Illus. 42. The Challenge scroll saw is similar to the Fleetwood, but has a heavier double-grooved driving wheel that carried a ⅜-inch round belt. The table featured a patented hollow ball joint tilting system. Other features included a lathe, emery wheel vertical drilling attachment and a dust blower. Also called the Boss saw by some merchants, this saw was produced by the Seneca Mfg. Co. of Seneca, New York around 1879. It had a 16-inch throat.

Illus. 44. The Rival scroll saw (1880) was one of the first to feature a vertical drilling attachment. Its optional lathe attachment handled stock 4 inches in diameter by only 9 inches in length.

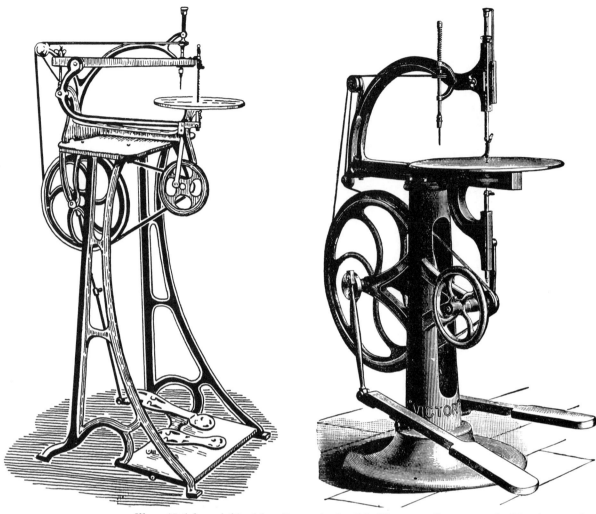

Illus. 45 (above left). Advertisements for this Victor scroll saw stated: "Tension can be adjusted with utmost nicety." It was also claimed that the saw had the best blade clamp. Illus. 46 (above right). The Victor industrial scroll saw, patented about 1879 for steam or foot power, was a large-capacity machine that cut stock 3 inches thick with 8-inch blades. It had a 24-inch throat, a tilting table, and a sawdust blower. The double-foot treadles were operated with a walking motion that produced about 800 strokes per minute. A lathe attachment with a 29-inch bed was also available.

trial use, and others were developed primarily for home use. Illus. 47 shows a novel, combination scroll saw-circular saw machine. The circular saw was of very small diameter and was intended only for very light sawing.

Illus. 48–50 show some of the first Barnes saws operated by foot treadles. The Velocipedes saw had a bicycle-like operation that was incorporated in both the lighter and heavier saws. (See Illus. 51–55.)

Other foot-powered saws that appeared in the 1870s and later include the Excelsior (Illus. 56), the Goodell Scroll Saw and Lathe Combination (Illus. 57), the New American (Illus. 58), the Clinton (Illus. 59), the Stafford (Illus. 60), and Pomeroy's House Saw (Illus. 61). Gardner's foot-powered saw (not illustrated) features a very large wooden table and two heavy flywheels that perpetuate inertial energy into the driving system.

Other names that are either associated with a manufacturer or identify certain mod-

Illus. 47. This 1872 Combined Machine, a product of the W. F. & John Barnes, Co., of Rockford, Illinois, worked as a scroll saw and circular saw.

Illus. 49. The No. 7 Scroll Saw, Improved, was manufactured by the W. F. & John Barnes Co.

Illus. 48. This foot-powered scroll saw was introduced by Barnes in 1872; it was their No. 7 model. The model shown here has a vertical hickory stick (secured to the rear leg) which serves as a spring return.

Illus. 50. This large-size Barnes foot-powered saw is of the same size and capacity as the company's Velocipede No. 2 saw. Ordinary operation produced from 800 to 1,200 cutting strokes per minute. This machine had a 24-inch throat and carried a 7-inch blade.

Illus. 51. Art that appeared in advertising for the No. 1 Amateur Saw manufactured by the Barnes Co. in 1872. This saw cut stock up to 1½ inches in thickness, and had a throat capacity of 18 inches. The ads claimed that "all muscles of the limbs are brought into healthful exercise which should be a good consideration when selecting a machine," and that "many a boy has been saved from vice by his growing interest in working with tools."

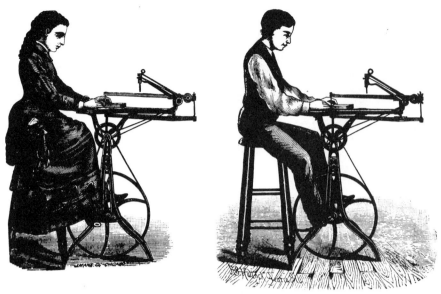

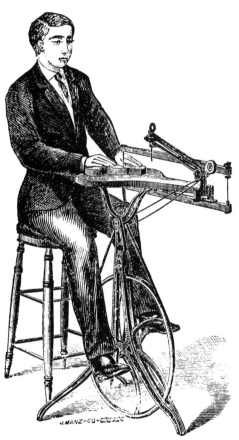

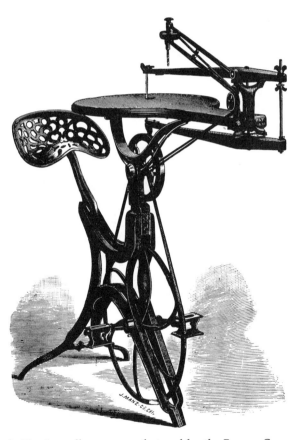

Illus. 52 (above left). The Velocipede No. 1 scroll saw, manufactured by the Barnes Co., was strictly for amateurs. An 1876 advertisement claimed: "A girl can manage it with ease from the first hour." The Velocipede (bikelike operation) permitted up to 2,000 reciprocations per minute. It had an 18-inch throat. Illus. 53 (above right). The pre-1880 model of the Velocipede No. 2 scroll saw, manufactured by the W. F. & John Barnes Co. Note the plain-drive belt.

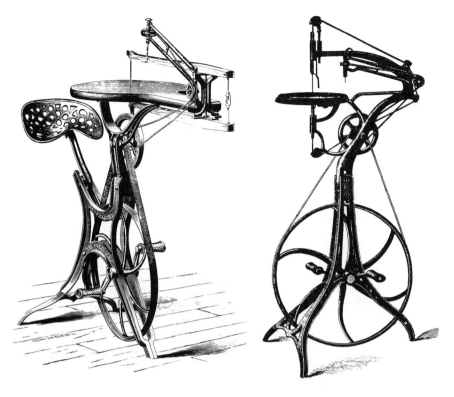

Illus. 54 (far left). The Barnes Velocipede No. 2 scroll saw could cut stock 3 inches thick at the rate of 1 foot per minute. This improved version had the perforated drive belt, which was made after 1880. The drilling attachment did not rotate until lowered to the work, which placed tension on the belts. The rate of speed varied between 800 to 1,200 strokes per minute. It carried a 7-inch blade, and had a 24-inch throat capacity. Illus. 55 (left). The No. 6 Amateur Saw, also called the Velocipede No. 6, was manufactured by the Barnes Co. and had a 16-inch throat.

Illus. 56 (far left). The Excelsior No. 2 scroll saw had a 16-inch bed lathe. Illus. 57 (left). The Goodell Scroll Saw and Lathe Companion was a product of the 1880s and 1890s. Note the grinding wheel and the horizontal drill at the left.

Illus. 58. The New American scroll saw, sold by A. H. Pomeroy, had some unique features that can be found in modern scroll saws. The lower arm could be adjusted rearward to improve sawing efficiency. The saw had a 20-inch throat capacity. As shown in the illustration, guides "B" and "B-1" prevented sideways motion, "C" was a tensioning lever, "H" was a air pump which gave a blast of air with each downward stroke of the arm that flowed into "F," the blower. A vertical drill table advanced the work to the bit with a lever, as shown at "E." Plus, this saw had a tilting table and optional lathe attachment.

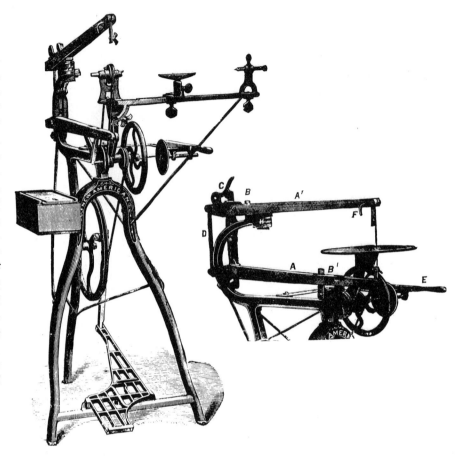

Illus. 59. (right). The Clinton scroll saw was produced around 1879. Illus. 60 (far right). The Stafford scroll saw, produced in 1879, was designed with a revolutionary blade clamping system that speed blade-threading operations for fretwork. The blade worked in a system of slots above and below the table with a reciprocating blade-clamp mechanism. The company's advertisement stated that the blade is "fastened only at the top and need not be unfastened again until necessary to change the blade."

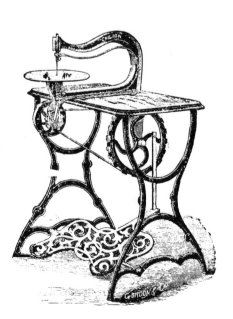

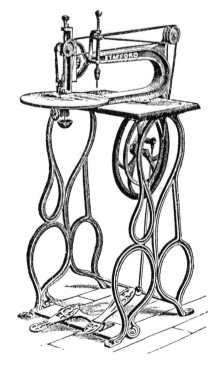

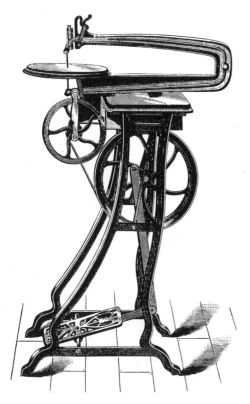

Illus. 61. The 1894 Improved House Saw, sold by A. H. Pomeroy, of Hartford, Connecticut, featured a revolutionary one-piece arm with a swing (throat capacity) of 17¾ inches. It sold for $10.00 and could be fitted with a wood lathe attachment that had a swing, between centers, of 4½ inches in diameter by 12 inches long.

Illus. 62. This treadle, made by Hobbies Ltd. of England, was also sold in the United States well into the 20th century. (Photo courtesy of Henry Aldinger)

els of early foot-power saws are Imperial, Wilds, Sears, Beach, Bentel, Bush, Griffin, Lewis, Plummer, Walker, Wright & Smith, E. O. Chase, New Giant, Triumph, and Victory. Hobbies Limited of England also sold a treadle saw in the United States well into the 20th century. (See Illus. 62.)

Various devices were developed in an attempt to make foot-powered energy more efficient. One item that was quite popular was the heavy foot wheels shown in Illus. 63. Water- and steam-powered factories ran many machines simultaneously by means of pulleys and belts from long line shafts that ran throughout the factory.

At that time, "water motors" were also available to individually drive light machinery, including scroll saws and sewing ma-

chines. These devices were less powerful and efficient than the foot wheels, and were not used often. They were driven by the force of a current of water that rushed from customary city mains and the like, and were similar in principle to the typical early water wheel. (See Illus. 64.) Large water motors with wheels of up to 24 inches in diameter and total weights of 650 pounds were available to power passenger and freight elevators, dynamos for electric lights, and to run heavy machine tools of all kinds.

Two hand-powered saws that probably date back to the 1920s are shown in Illus. 65 and 66.

In the early 1920s small electric motors for individual machines were becoming more widely accepted, even though the induction

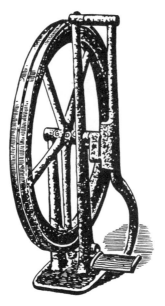

Illus. 63 (above left and center). Foot wheels were used in the late 1880s to run all sorts of machinery, including lathes, scroll saws, and even dental tools. These heavy wheels, some as large as 18 inches in diameter, had a grooved face for a round belt or could be used with a flat belt. Illus. 64 (above right). The Tuerk water motor was used to run sewing machines, scroll saws, telephone generators, and similar light machinery. The water motor ran at full speed a scroll saw that could cut wood 1½ inches thick. To do this, it operated at water pressure of 25–30 pounds, which consumed 50 gallons of water per hour. The motor wheel diameter was only 4 inches.

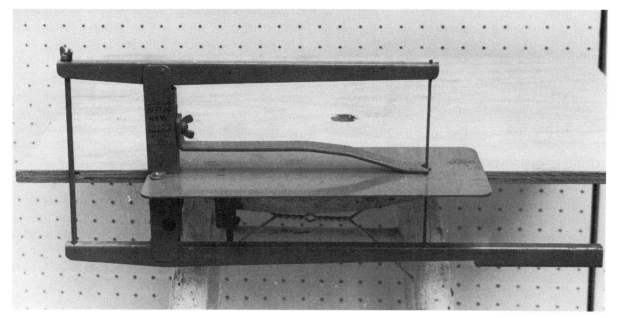

Illus. 65. This Jiffy Saw by Dupli-Craft was made in Mountain View, California. It was a hand-powered saw that clamped to the edge of a table or bench. Note the hold-down, which made it easier to feed the wood to the saw with one hand. (Photo courtesy of Henry Aldinger)

Illus. 66. This Buster Brown scroll saw carried pin-end blades. It may have been offered as a premium with the purchase of shoes. (Photo courtesy of Henry Aldinger)

motor had been in existence since 1888. Electric motor-powered machines were not quickly purchased because rural America did not get electricity for quite a while. In fact, some rural areas didn't receive electricity until the late 1930s. Two early saws that were probably designed to be used with electric motors that have belted drives are shown in Illus. 67 and 68.

In 1921, Carl Moberg of Chicago invented a crank-operated scroll saw for boys. Around 1925 Herbert Tautz, a manufacturer of sewing machines in Milwaukee, started to produce it. (See Illus. 69 and 70.) In the years following the Great Depression, this production effort expanded into the Delta Mfg. Co., and the famous heavy rigid-arm jigsaw eventually came into existence. This saw has been a standard school-shop item from the 1930s up until today.

Illus. 71 and 72 show two early electrified scroll saws. Illus. 73–75 show two early (non-electrified) industrial scroll saws. These saws, like the rigid-arm 24-inch saw Delta,

were actually called jigsaws because of their spring-type blade-tensioning mechanisms.

Scroll saws did not undergo a further major change in design and manufacture until Helmut Abel of Germany patented the Hegner constant-tension scroll saw in 1974. (See Illus. 76.) This scroll saw—a high-tech, well-engineered product of modern metal alloys that was electrically driven—is a vastly improved version of the constant-tension saws of the 1800s.

Many other manufacturers have since rushed to claim a piece of this huge and still expanding market. In 1982, R. B. Industries of Missouri became the first American company to enter the market. Since then, many new saws have been introduced. The *Scroll Saw Handbook*, 1986 Sterling Publishing Co., describes the contemporary saws manufactured up to the publication of the book. A number of the more recent "new" saws and other commercial innovations, some specifically of interest to those contemplating fretwork, are discussed in the next chapter.

Illus. 67. This Walker-Turner saw dates back to the 1920s. It has wooden arms and carries pin-end blades. (Photo courtesy of Henry Aldinger)

Illus. 68. This saw, which dates back to about 1920, carried pin-end blades. (Photo courtesy of Henry Aldinger)

Illus. 69. (above left). Shown here is the first scroll saw manufactured by Herbert Tautz, in Milwaukee, Wisconsin, which eventually became the Delta Power Tool Co., and which today is Delta International Machinery Corporation. The frame carrying the blade moves up and down with the operation of the hand crank. The lower frame is a hold-down that is adjustable to stock thickness. Wording on the cast base reads: "Made in USA, Pat. AUG 21–23, Delta Specialty Co., Milwaukee, Wis., American Boy Scroll Saw." Illus. 70 (above right). A close-up look at the grooved cross-head, in which the inner end of a crank (extending from the shaft) rides. When the hand crank revolves, the cross-head carrying the saw frame is driven up and down on the two vertical guide posts. This basic system for converting rotary motion to a reciprocating action is still employed in the rigid arm, 24-inch Delta jigsaws manufactured today.

Illus. 71. An early electric saw, name brand unknown. Note how the saw frame design formed the motor end plates. (Photo courtesy of Henry Aldinger)

Illus. 72 (right). Fay's early-industrial scroll saw was driven by line shafts from water or steam power. Note the ceiling-mounted, overhead straining mechanism which provided an unlimited throat capacity. The blade holder moved in vertical guides, which were reciprocated by the wheel and pitman action. Illus. 73 (far right). This early-industrial jigsaw employed an overhead spring system to maintain suitable blade tension. Note the automatic blower used to remove sawdust.

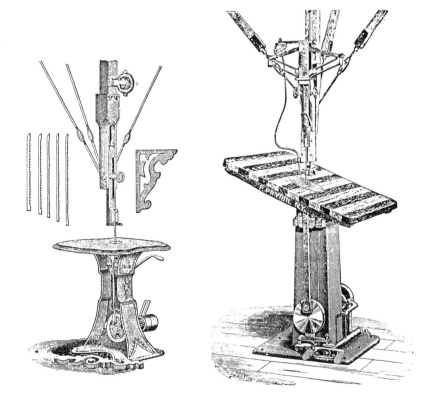

Illus. 74. This 1927 version of an early electrified scroll saw produced by the W. F. & John Barnes Co. did not become popular because competitive saws such as Delta featured cast iron rather than wood tables. This machine featured 7-inch blades, a ¼ h.p. motor, a 24-inch throat capacity and a boring attachment. It cut stock 2 inch in thickness at 900 strokes per minute. It also carried a 4-inch-diameter emery wheel.

Illus. 75. This industrial-quality jigsaw (scroll saw) was designed to do large Victorian fretwork on a production basis. This machine, a Superior brand, No. 46, was manufactured circa 1882. An electric motor was added in 1906. The blade tension consists of leather belts connected to a large spring. The table and power rod are of wood construction. This machine was manufactured by the Jones Superior Machine Co., of Chicago, Illinois. Note the cast figurehead at the top. (Photo courtesy of Don Thomas)

Illus. 76. Helmut Abel of Germany is the 1974 patent holder for the Hegner line of scroll saws which inspired a resurgence in scroll saws and scroll-sawing activities of all kinds.

Illus. 77. The Multi-Max 2 shown here was Hegner's first scroll saw, but was shortly followed by the company's famous Polymax. Now they manufacture an expanded line of saws, one with the capability to cut stock up to 2¾ inches thick, and which has a variable-speed drive.

II
HAND TOOLS, SCROLL SAWS, AND BLADES

There are very few basic necessities required for getting started in fretwork. An inexpensive saw frame and a drill are all one needs to take up hand fretwork. However, from this point on, there is virtually no limit to the equipment you can buy.

You may eventually decide to buy a scroll saw. Today, there is a very large, ever-expanding selection of scroll saws to choose from. They vary greatly in price.

There are many factors to consider when you are selecting a scroll saw. You have to have an understanding of the blades available, as well as the most recent and improved scroll saws to arrive on the market. These subjects are explored in this chapter. To avoid repetition, only those machines that have been manufactured or improved since 1986 and the publication of the *Scroll Saw Handbook* will be examined. (If you want to learn about basic scroll-sawing techniques, as well as marquetry and inlaying techniques, also see the *Scroll Saw Handbook*.) Do not assume that just because they are being discussed, they are being endorsed. Also discussed and illustrated are ways that certain machines can be made more adaptable to fretwork and/or scroll sawing in general.

With the information presented here, you will be able to determine if a particular scroll saw is suitable for fret cutting and meets both your individual sawing requirements and general ones. This is a determination that will vary from person to person.

HAND TOOLS

The hand-held fretsaw frame is still available as an alternative to power sawing. (See Illus. 78.) It was the first type of saw ever used for fretwork, and although it is now made differently, it is still fairly popular. The hand frame can be helpful in certain situations. Some fretworkers may want to make part or all of their projects with a hand frame so that they can feel that their work is, in fact, "hand"-made. Prior to his death, professional fretworker Lawrence Boehner did all of his work with a hand-held frame. Some of his pieces are shown in Chapter X.

The most popular hand fretsaw frames available today have a throat depth of approximately 12 inches. These frames consist of a C arm and two blade clamps, and take pinless 5-inch blades like those used for scroll saws. The blade is kept rigid because the spring-steel arms are bent. When the blade is clamped, the spring in the arms provides tension to the fine blade(s) it carries.

Smaller-sized frames called jeweller saw frames are available with throat sizes that range from 2½ to 8 inches. These frames are usually adjustable for blade length, so shorter or broken blades can be used. A hand-held frame called the coping saw is also available. This type of saw has a throat of approximately 5 inches, and the blade can be turned 360 degrees to permit sawing in any direction. However, the blades must have

41

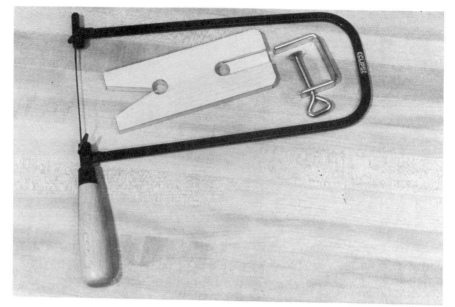

Illus. 78. A typical-hand held saw frame. Also shown is a v-block and clamp which comprise what is called a "cutting table." This table supports the workpiece as it is being sawn.

ends with pins. These blades are not made in small sizes, which limits the use of this saw for fine fretwork.

If you are going to use a hand fretsaw frame, you need a "cutting table" which is also called a "bird's mouth" saw table or a coping saddle. This is usually nothing more than a commercial or homemade V-cut board and a clamp that secures it to a table or workbench. (See Illus. 78.) Cutting tables vary in size from 2½ inches × 7 inches to approximately 8 inches × 12 inches. Hardwood ½ or ¾ inch thick is the most suitable wood to use. The board has a V-shaped aperture, and an approximately ⅝-inch-diameter circle at the point of the V. You can cut in a smaller size aperture to provide support for extremely fine cutting. If the aperture is too large, the piece being sawn does not have adequate support; if the aperture is too small, the blade is restricted in its cutting.

The cutting table is often secured to a table or bench with one or two clamps and with the upper arms, which lie in grooves and keep the clamp(s) below the surface. You can also secure the table with bolts, screws, or glue, or set the cutting board into a recess that you have carved or routed into the surface of the workbench to ensure that the cutting table surface and the bench surfaces are flush with each other. This is an ideal way to support large, and very fragile, fret cuttings.

Besides sawing, there are other uses for the cutting table. It can be used to support the work when you are "touching up" a sawn piece with a knife, file, or an abrasive stick.

You need a *drill* to drill holes into the waste areas of the work so that you can thread the blade through to cut out the inside openings. This is sometimes called piercing work. The holes are called "saw gates" by some sawers.

The first tool you would think to use in this situation is obviously a drill press, but there are alternatives. A portable electric hand drill will work fine, as will other nonelectric drills such as the spiral drill or Archimedean drill (named after the Greek mathematician and inventor born in 287 BC). (See Illus. 79.) The downward stroke of the bobbin causes the spiral stock of the spiral drill to turn rapidly, thus rotating the bit. Two other hand-powered drills are the carpenter's "push drill" and a hand drill with a hand crank.

The bits used to drill fretwork saw blade holes (or saw gates) vary in diameter from ¹⁄₁₆-inch and smaller for very delicate work to ⅛-inch and larger.

The Moto-Tool, made by Dremel, or similar high-speed rotary tools can also be an asset to the fretworker. (See Illus. 80.) Not

42

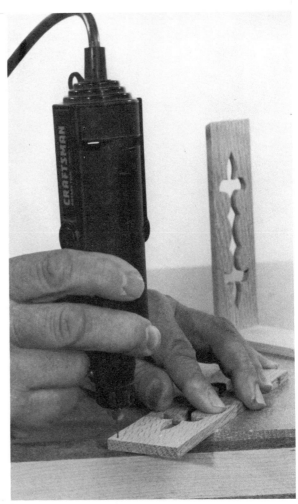

Illus. 79 (above left). The spiral or Archimedean drill is inexpensive, and cuts almost all thin materials quickly. Illus. 80 (above right). The high-speed rotary tool is ideal for drilling "saw gates" and small screw and nail pilot holes, as shown here, in assembly work.

only are they used to drill holes for interior cutouts, they can be very useful for drilling pilot holes for nails and screws in fine assembly work. Different size collets are available with which you can use ⅟₃₂-, ⅟₁₆-, ³⁄₃₂-, and ⅛-inch standard-twist drill bits.

Ray Lawler of The Tool Company has devised a very useful homemade device that incorporates the high-speed rotary tool as a power drilling unit on a spring-loaded arm that's ideal for production work. This device is, in fact, better than an expensive drill press. (See Illus. 394–397, starting on page 188.) High-speed rotary tools can also be fitted with a wide variety of cutters and form-

ing tools that are useful in carving frets and other decorative detailing.

Small files or rasps are useful for touching-up sawing imperfections. There are needle file sets available which include the following shapes: round, half round, square, three square, flat, knife, equalling, crossing, slitting, barette, joint, and marking. (See Illus. 81.) Obtain the needle file that gives you the coarsest cut possible. This would be the No. 0-cut needle file, in comparison to the finer Nos. 2-, 3-, and 4-cut needle files. There are also other individual file and rasp sets available.

Filing to correct imperfect cutting should

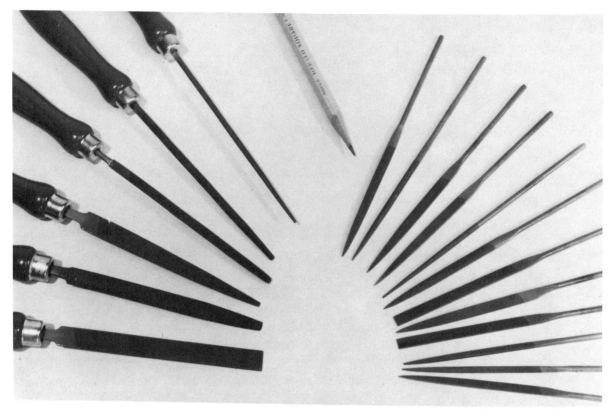

Illus. 81. Shown here is a set of files with larger handles and a finer set of 12 needle files. Dowels can be used as handles for the needle files.

not be considered an easy or viable alternative to good sawing work. If you saw adequately, and the scroll saw performs to the normal standards, you will not have to use files or rasps because the saw itself will cut the surface smoothly enough.

Miscellaneous tools commonly needed and found in most home shops include such items as a knife for cleaning up sawn edges, a ruler, scissors, an awl, a screwdriver, and a small hand plane. A small, light hammer is handy for driving small brads or nails. Also needed is a small hand saw, a mitre box (or some other means of cutting wood to length and squaring ends, etc.), and a means of cutting panels of plywood or solid lumber into workable sizes. Some light clamps for assembly work may also be useful and convenient. It would be helpful if you have access to

larger shop tools such as a table saw, sander, etc., but, as stated previously, many of these tools are actually not necessary. Also helpful are drawing and layout tools such as plastic 45 and 30-60-degree triangles, French curves, a compass, and various templates with circles, squares, or ellipses.

Finally, a very useful homemade device called a "shooting board" is highly recommended for squaring, joining, and fitting together panels in any of a wide variety of straight or angular joints. A shooting board is almost essential when you are truing or accurately fitting very small pieces together—especially if you're not blessed with expensive precision power tools such as jointers, table saws, and/or mitre-cutting devices. Details for making and using a shooting board are given on page 153, Chapter VII.

SCROLL SAWS

The number and types of scroll saws available to the home woodcrafter are constantly increasing. At first thought, you might assume that you can do fretwork or make projects that involve a good amount of piercing or cutout openings more expediently with modern, highly-tensioned scroll saws. This is not necessarily so!

The majority of the scroll saws available today generally lack two distinct features that are very important to the modern day fretworker. The first feature, which is extremely critical, is whether the saw blade can be threaded through a drilled hole and reclamped quickly. This sounds easy, but surprisingly it will take you considerably longer to thread a blade on a modern saw than one on a saw that has old wooden arms and a crude clamping and tensioning system.

Imagine making a project with over 4,000 inside cutouts, like Carl Weckhorst's clock project, of which a partial view is shown on page 211. You will spend most of your time on a project of this magnitude threading and unthreading, so every second saved is indeed desirable. It even gets frustrating when you use an expensive top-of-the-line saw on a much smaller scale, such as when sawing a simple project that requires only about a dozen blade threadings. This is because you are continually going through the procedures of switching off the power, untensioning, unclamping, and threading the blade, reclamping and retensioning the blade, turning the power switch back on, and then finally sawing the cut out, before starting the routine all over again.

The second feature that is important is a much slower blade stroke speed than is usual. Beginners and most experienced sawers will find saws with slower speeds easier to control, and will find that when using a slow-cutting saw, they can make precise, accurate cuts more easily when working thin materials. True, faster-cutting strokes are best for sawing stock ½-1½ inch thick.

Many of the popular or top-rated scroll saws have only one high speed. Others have either a variable-speed control or a step pulley and a belted drive that can slow the blade down.

The person who used the foot treadle on the late nineteenth-century Velocipede saws could slow down the cutting speed to make a precise curve or a sharp turn, and could then speed it up again on the "straightaways" and the more gradual curves. Consequently, a foot-powered saw was ideal because the person could establish optimum speed instinctively exactly where and when it was needed during the course of a particular saw cut without having to remove his hands or stop to change a belt, dial, or the electronic control.

Only one pedal, foot-powered saw is available today that we know of. It is a cast-aluminum reproduction of the popular Barnes No. 2 Velocipede scroll saw that was patented in 1871. (See Illus. 82.) This saw is manufactured and distributed by The Tool Company, 5271 Raintree Parkway, Lee's Summit, Missouri 64082.

Also available from The Tool Company are some of the same Velocipede castings and maple wooden arms with which the typical do-it-yourselfer can make a motorized saw kit. (See Illus. 83 and 84.) This saw kit, like the Velocipede saw, has a 24-inch throat, a 1⅛-inch blade stroke, and is capable of cutting wood up to 2 inches in thickness. Both the Tool Company's Velocipede reproduction saw and its kit saws have identical blade clamps. The upper clamp employs a quick thumbscrew system (Illus. 85), but the lower clamps require an Allen wrench, which is somewhat inconvenient.

An English company, Peter Gee Products, makes a fretsaw of stamped sheet-metal parts. The saw and its essential features are shown in Illus. 86–88. It has an 18-inch throat capacity and carries standard 5-inch blades in typical gimbal-type blade clamps.

The Microlux Multi-Saw, shown in Illus. 89–92, is a saw for a model maker or some-

Illus. 82. This reproduction of the Barnes No. 2 Velocipede scroll saw is manufactured in cast aluminum by the Tool Company of Missouri. The saw has a 24-inch throat capacity and carries all 5-inch plain-end blades.

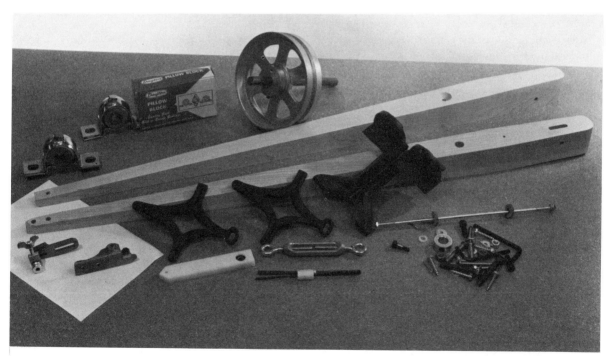

Illus. 83. The components of the Tool Company's do-it-yourself scroll saw kit. You must provide your own motor, motor pulley, belt, electrical switching components, and wood for the table and stand.

 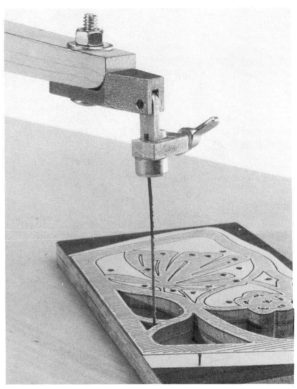

Illus. 84 (above left). One version of the completed and assembled scroll saw kit offered by the Tool Company. Check or modify the table plans to make accessibility to the lower blade clamp more convenient. This saw is shown with an optional 8-inch disc sander accessory that fits the pulley shaft. Illus. 85 (above right). This upper blade clamp is standard on the Tool Company's Velocipede reproduction saw and on its motorized scroll-saw kits.

Illus. 86. The Peter Gee Products scroll saw is made in England.

Illus. 87 (above left). This view of the Peter Gee Benchmaster scroll saw shows it from its opposite side. Illus. 88 (above right). A closer look at the formed sheet metal arms, the saw blade clamps, and the driving mechanism on the Benchmaster scroll saw.

Illus. 89. The Microlux Multi-Saw. This mini-scroll saw has a 9-inch throat, a 6¼ × 6¼-inch rigid table, and carries standard 5-inch plain-end blades.

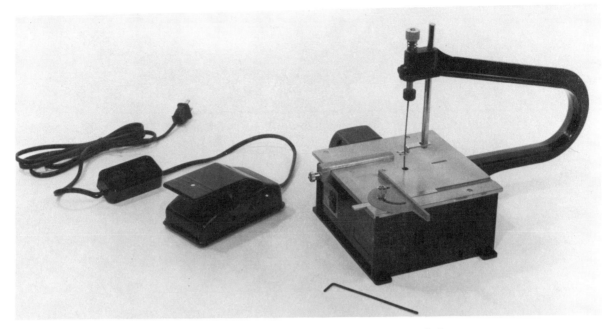

Illus. 90. The Microlux Multi-Saw comes with a variable-speed foot-operated rheostat with which you can change blade speed at will during the cut.

Illus. 91 (above left). The Microlux Multi-Saw is designed for model and miniature work. Note the rip fence and mitre gauge accessories. Illus. 92 (above right). A close-up look at the blade clamp (chuck), which requires an allen wrench, and the tensioning knob above on the Microlux Multi-Saw.

Illus. 93. The new Sears 16-inch Craftsman scroll saw has a constant-tension design and carries pin-type blades.

one who cuts miniature pieces. This compact unit will cut 2-inch-thick balsa, ¾-inch-thick pine, ½-inch-thick plywood, ¹⁄₁₆-inch-thick aluminum and ¹⁄₃₂-inch-thick brass. It is very small, measuring only 9 inches × 13 inches overall, and is sold with a rip fence, a mitre gauge, and a variable-speed foot-operated rheostat. It uses all standard 5-inch plain-end blades and holds them in blade chucks (top and bottom) that are secured with an Allen wrench. The Microlux Multi-Saw is manufactured by the Japanese and sold in the United States by Micro-Mark, 340 Snyder Avenue, Berkeley Heights, New Jersey 07922.

The Sears 16-inch Craftsman scroll saw (Illus. 93) performs much better than the Walking Beam saw Sears introduced several years ago. This new constant-tension saw also costs considerably less, but it has some limitations. The only blades that can be used with the saw are 5-inch medium or fine pin-end blades. (The designations medium or fine essentially pertain to the sharpness of the radius the blades cut.)

The blade on a Sears 16-inch saw can be changed, threaded, and tensioned very quickly in comparison to many of the other saws that require an Allen wrench and other

tools. With the blade holders available you can install the blade to cut from either the front or from the side of the machine. (See Illus. 94.) The pin-end blades need holes ¹¹⁄₆₄ inch in diameter when you are threading a fine-cut blade, and holes ³⁄₁₆ inch in diameter

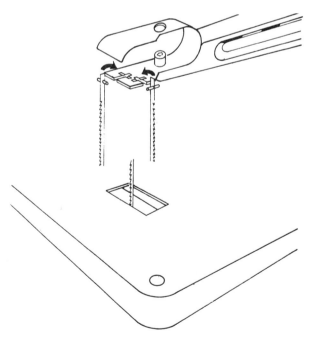

Illus. 94. Blades can be mounted to cut from the front (as usual) or to cut from the side, in band saw fashion.

when you are threading a medium-cut blade. You can slip the fine blade through a 5/32-inch-diameter hole if you reduce the length of the blade pin slightly by carefully touching it against a grinder. This saw can be used to do a lot of fine fretwork with the exception of extremely fine and delicate profiles that can only be handled with the smallest plain end blades available.

Illus. 95 and 96 show a way to increase a blade's tight radius-sawing capabilities by using a diamond hone, stone, or fine file to

Illus. 96. This tight-radius-curve cut in ¾-inch oak was made with a Sears 16-inch saw that had a modified, fine blade.

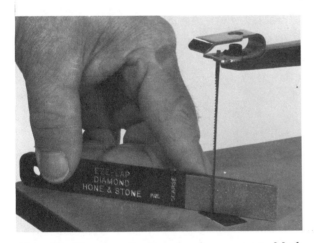

Illus. 95. Here is a tip from band-saw expert, Mark Duginske: When you round the sharp rear edges of the blade, as shown, you can make tighter than usual turns with any saw.

round the sharp back corners of the blade.

The Dremel Hobby Saw (Illus. 97) is another saw that utilizes pin-end blades. Like the Sears saw, only coarse or fine blades can be used. Unlike the blades used for the Sears saw, those used for the Dremel are only 3 inches in total length. (Refer to Illus. 100 on page 70.)

Illus. 98–104 show how to use the Dremel saw to cut much finer fretwork than could be normally done. Simply reduce the size of the blade's pin end so that it can be threaded through a smaller hole than usual.

Illus. 97. The Dremel saw is limited in the type of very fine fretwork it can do, but with some modification to the blades, its capability for making fine fretwork cuts in thin material can be dramatically increased.

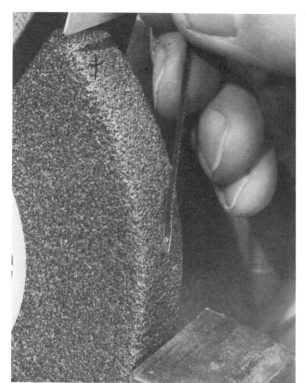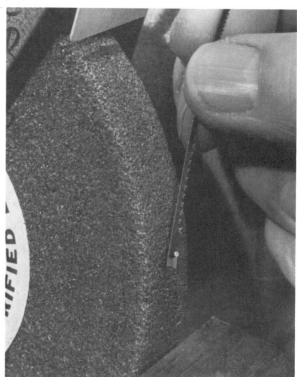

Illus. 98 (above left). Grind the end of the blade to decrease its width. Illus. 99 (above right). Grind the pins shorter.

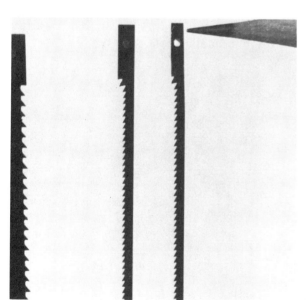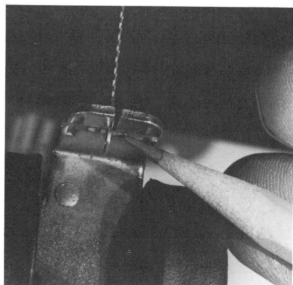

Illus. 100 (above left). Shown on the right is a modified fine Dremel blade; compare it to the same unaltered blade at center and the coarse Dremel blade on the left. Illus. 101 (above right). The shorter pins are still well supported in the blade holder.

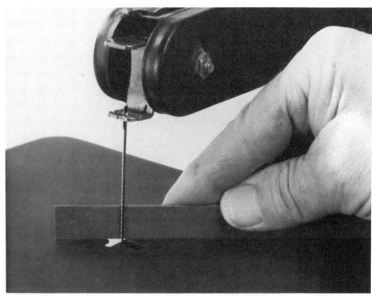

Illus. 102 (left). Best of all, the blade entry hole for the fine Dremel blade is reduced from a ⁵/₃₂-inch to a ³/₃₂ or ⁷/₆₄-inch hole; this permits internal designs of much finer detail to be sawn. Illus. 103 (above). If you round the back corners of the blade, you will be able to make even sharper turns.

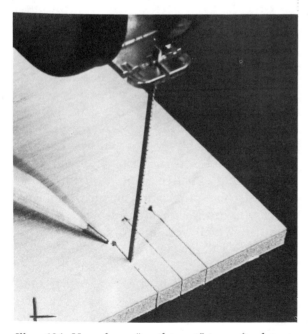

Illus. 104. Very sharp, "on-the-spot" turns (such as on this ¼-inch thick, softer material) are possible to the degree that the blade can exit on the inbound cut with only a minimum of rubbing or burning at the turn-around area.

The blade on a Dremel saw can be threaded and unthreaded very quickly because no threaded blade clamps or tensioning devices are involved. The two principal limitations of this saw are its inability to cut thick and hard materials and, because of its blade's width, its limitation in doing very fine and intricate work. Otherwise, the Dremel saw is very satisfactory for sawing particular fretted patterns in thin materials, whether they are hard or soft.

The new Delta 15-inch scroll saw (Illus. 105) closely resembles a number of other saws of essentially the same design like, for example, saws by the following manufacturers: AMT and JET (both saws described in the *Scroll Saw Handbook*), Penn State (this company's saw has a blower), Grizzly, Sunhill, and Bridgewood. These saws incorporate the pivoting-blade clamp features and the rocking parallelogram design that Hegner introduced in the late 1970s.

The general specifications for the Delta 15-

Illus. 105. The Delta 15-inch model is very similar to a number of other saws that simulate Hegner's pivoting blade suspension and rocking parallelogram design. Although certain modifications can be made by the owner to improve saw performance, it is questionable if saws of this type in general are conducive to highly detailed fretwork, for two reasons: they cut thin materials very quickly, and blades cannot be changed conveniently on them.

inch home-shop scroll saw are as follow: a 2-inch thickness-cutting capability, a ⅞-inch cutting stroke, a weight of 37 pounds, a 1.6 amp motor, and the capacity to cut at the rate of 1,725 cutting strokes per minute. It uses 5-inch standard blades. Saws of this design all have fairly good cutting capabilities considering their comparative low purchase prices, but you can do certain things to improve their efficiency. (See Illus. 106.) First, mount the saw to a workbench or onto another wooden base that can be clamped to the workbench or table. Place rubber washers or foam under the saw to minimize vibration and noise. Do not overtighten the mounting bolts, and leave some cushioning space so that the motion and sound can be absorbed.

Zach Etheridge of Highland Hardware, 1045 N. Highland Ave., N.E., Atlanta, Georgia 30306, has come up with a great idea for the owners of saws like the Delta 15-inch saw that will improve the saw's overall performance. Simply make a "pocket" block that holds the blade clamps steadily as you insert

the blade and tighten the clamp with the allen wrench provided. (See Illus. 107 and 108.) You are in effect devising a blade-clamping system that is similar to the ones attached to the edge of Hegner saw tables.

Highland Hardware offers a publication, *User's Guide for the Delta 15" Scroll Saw*, that contains other helpful hints. This booklet gives instructions and full-size patterns for making a workable hold-down arm system. The plastic hold-downs that come with these saws are not effective. They function better as guards. The publication also lists kits with which you can make a hold-down and an air pump to which you would add a sawdust blower. (See Illus. 144.)

Hegner now makes available a conversion or upgrade kit that is specifically marketed for the users of the Delta 15-inch saw and other saws that are similar in design to the Hegner saws. Included in this kit are instructions, blade clamps, a "Tuff" wrench, a blade clamp holder that can be mounted to the edge of the saw table, and the necessary mounting screws. (See Illus. 109.)

Illus. 106. Two simple improvements can be made to saws of this type: One, mount the saw to a workbench or to another wood base which can be clamped to a workbench with rubber washers or foam padding under the saw, to dampen vibration. Two, make and mount hardwood "pocket" blocks; these blocks hold the blade clamps steadily when you tighten them with an allen wrench.

Illus. 107. A closer look at the blade clamping "pocket." The opening can be sawn through a hardwood block (of the appropriate thickness) with the saw itself and then mounted with screws, as shown. Another approach is to chisel a pocket into the surface of your workbench.

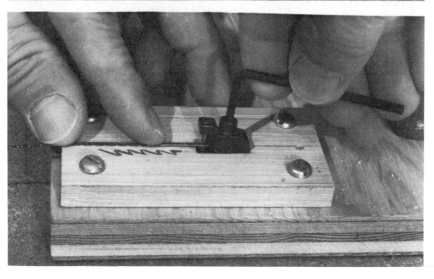

Illus. 108. The blade clamp "pocket" should be of the appropriate depth so that when a blade is placed on the surface it will slide directly into the slotted opening of the metal blade clamp, as shown.

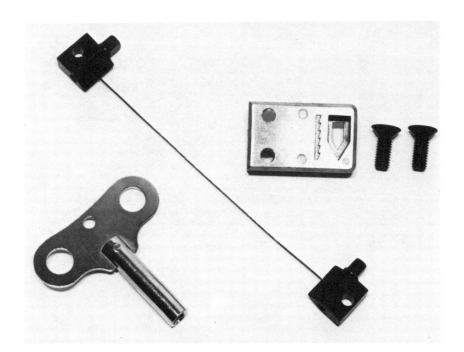

Illus. 109. Advanced Machinery Imports, Ltd., now sells a saw upgrade or conversion kit which consists of the company's blade clamps, blade holder, etc.

Illus. 110 and 111 show how to make a blade clamp holder, or "pocket," for Hegner blade clamps. The Hegner conversion or "upgrade" kits are available in the United States through Advanced Machinery Imports, Ltd., Box 312, New Castle, Delaware 19720. AMI also makes a blade-clamp upgrade kit for the new Superscroll 18-inch scroll saw. (See Illus. 112.) The Superscroll is an imported saw sold by American Machinery Sales, Inc., P.O. Box 5285, Marshallton, Delaware 19808.

A new Hegner scroll saw named the Multimax 18 has just arrived on the market to complement other Hegner models. In addition to an 18-inch throat, this new saw features a 2¾-inch maximum-cutting-thickness capacity and a dial-operated variable-speed control (standard equipment) that provides a blade speed that ranges from 400 to 1,480 strokes per minute. The blade suspension and other features are essentially the same as features on the other Multimax models.

Hegner has also recently introduced a "piercing pal" accessory, as shown in Illus. 113 and 114. The piercing pal is a blade-centering device that speeds up blade-threading operations when you are making internal cutouts as in fretwork. To use it, insert the top end of the blade into the blade clamp while the blade clamp remains tightly locked in the upper arm. This accessory is now available for use on all Multimax and Polymax saws.

Illus. 110. Trace around the slotted Hegner blade clamp. Carefully cut out the "pocket," saving the line to make a very close fit.

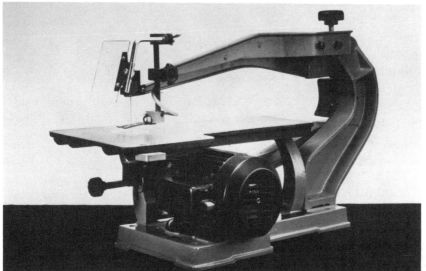

Illus. 111. Note the straight guide line and the saw teeth drawn on the surface. The teeth of the blade should face towards the "pocket" when you place the blade in the first of the two blade clamps. This will ensure that the screws of both blade clamps will face to the right side of the blade when the assembly is mounted on the arms of the saw.

Illus. 112. This 18-inch Superscroll scroll saw is of foreign manufacture, but is sold in this country by American Machinery Sales, Inc. It has a C-arm design, a ¾-inch stroke, a ⅛ h.p. direct drive, carries 5-inch blades, and will cut stock 1½ inches thick.

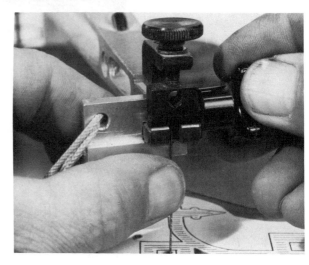

Illus. 113. (above left). Hegner's "piercing pal" is an aluminum accessory that fits behind the upper blade clamp to speed blade threading in fretwork. Illus. 114 (above right). The piercing pal, when inserted behind the blade clamp, aids in properly centering the blade within the blade clamp.

The Excalibur 24-inch scroll saw has also been improved. This extremely popular saw now has an "up-front" blade tensioning control that is a great advantage for those making frequent blade changes. In addition, this saw, though still available with a variable-speed motor drive, can also be ordered with a belted drive on which you mount your own ¼-horsepower motor. (See Illus. 115.) The belted-drive motor has three blade speeds: 600, 1,000, or 1,725 strokes per minute. Seyco Sales Co., 1414 Cranford Drive, P.O. Box 472749, Garland, Texas 75047, is the major United States affiliate for this Canadian-made line of scroll saws. Canadians can contact The Excalibur Machine and Tool Co., 3241 Kennedy Road, Scarborough, Ontario, Canada M1V2J9.

Another newcomer to the scroll-saw market is the Procut 20-scroll saw, manufactured by the Lancaster Machinery Co., 715 Fountain Ave., Lancaster, Pennsylvania 17601. (See Illus. 116.) This company, which claims that it is the "home of the original DeWalt Radial Arm Saw," gives the following specifi-

Illus. 116. The Pro-Cut 20-inch scroll saw is made by Lancaster Machinery Co., the "DeWalt Radial Arm Saw People."

cations for its new scroll saw: a 20-inch throat, a 1-inch stroke, a 2-inch maximum-cutting depth, a ⅛-horsepower motor with a 4-speed belted drive (800, 925, 1,000 and 1,160 spm), a 45-degree right and left table tilt, and a shipping weight of 70 pounds.

Shopsmith, which is well-known as a manufacturer of combination woodworking tools for the home shop, has recently introduced its version of a freestanding scroll saw. (See Illus. 117–119.) This machine, essentially of all cast-aluminum construction, has some distinct features (both good and bad) not usually found on other scroll saws. The provision for a shop vacuum hook-up is helpful, as is the well-designed combined speed control and power switching unit. (See Illus. 119.)

One major disadvantage of this saw when it is used for fine fretwork is that the blade must be fitted with blade clamps so precisely spaced apart that the manufacturer provides a separate jig just for this purpose. (See Illus. 120.) The numerous steps involved in changing and/or threading a blade to make inside cuts are very tedious and time-consuming. (See Illus. 121–125.)

Illus. 115. The Excalibur 24-inch saw also comes in a belt-drive model on which you can mount your own ¼ hp 1,725 rpm motor. A quick-change step pulley provides blade speeds of 500, 1,000, and 1,725 strokes per minute. The new models of this saw have an up-front blade-tensioning knob that is more convenient for the operator.

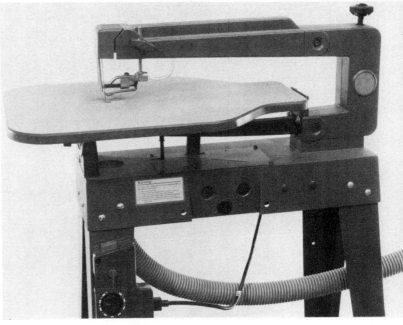

Illus. 117 (above left). This Shopsmith 20-inch scroll saw has an owner's shop vacuum hose connected to a dust port located directly under the blade. Illus. 118 (above right). A closer look at the Shopsmith scroll saw. This machine has a rocking parallelogram design, but at first look it resembles a rigid-arm jigsaw. Notice the sawdust port in the base and the hinged hood that covers the upper blade clamping mechanism.

Illus. 119. The Shopsmith scroll saw has combination speed control and power switching. In addition, the owner can plug his shop vacuum into the bottom of the control box so that it will turn on and off automatically with the saw switch. The control box also features a keyed lockout to prevent unauthorized operation of the saw.

Illus. 120. Shown here is the Shopsmith jig with which you can mount the blade clamps the precise distance from each other. First, place and clamp all the parts properly in the blade-mounting fixture, and then, use the allen wrench to tighten each clamp to the blade.

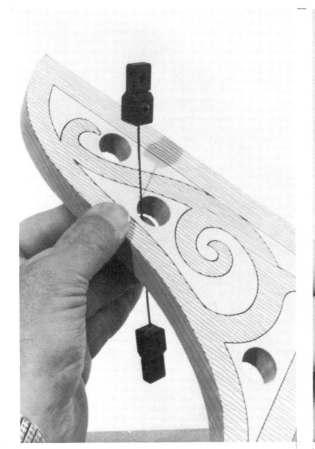

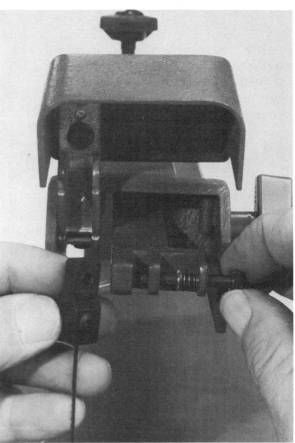

Illus. 121 (above left). The Shopsmith blade clamps shown here require at least a hole ¾-inch in diameter, as do many other saws, when you thread with both blade clamps secured to the blade. Illus. 122 (above right). A spring-loaded pin engages (into a hole) the blade clamp. Note the raised hood which pivots down to cover this entire mechanism.

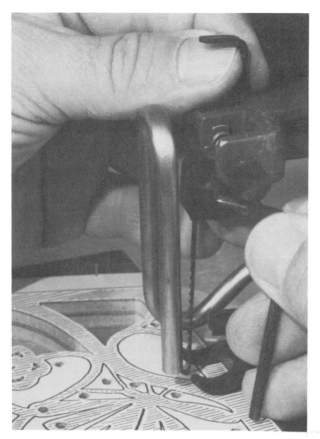
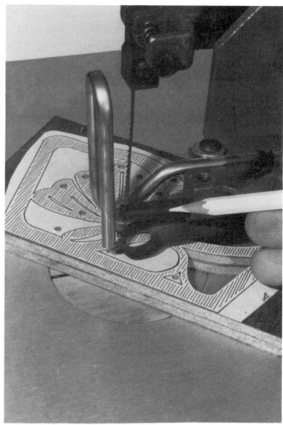

Illus. 123 (above left). Blade threading the Shopsmith scroll saw for fine fretwork. You must insert a shim behind the blade clamp to minimize movement when you use the allen wrench to release or secure the top blade clamp. Illus. 124 (above right). Once the blade is inserted through the saw gate (hole) of the workpiece, reinsert and secure it in the upper blade clamp. Tensioning is next. To tension a blade, you first have to consult a chart that reveals the particular number of "clicks" that correspond to the various sizes of blades that are listed according to Shopsmith's own part numbers. Then, adjust the v-notched blade back-up (at the pencil) and the hold-down to the stock thickness.

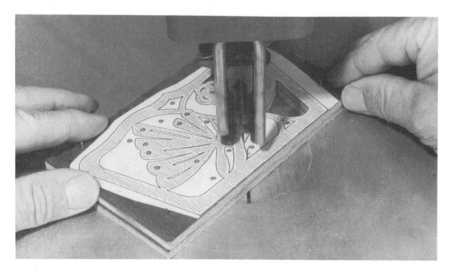

Illus. 125. An operator's view of the sawing of fine fretwork on a Shopsmith scroll saw. The sawdust blower tube is bent to also serve as a guard that protects both sides of the blade.

Another disadvantage is that for a scroll-saw user to tension a blade on a Shopsmith scroll saw he has to first consult a special chart to determine the amount of clicks (knob noises) that determine the blade he is using is adequately tensioned, and then count the clicks while tensioning the blade. One final disadvantage is that Shopsmith has incorporated so many safety features into its saw, that they sometimes are actually troublesome; this may, in fact, encourage the active user to remove them entirely.

Strong Tool Design Company now offers three new machines: a 20-inch model now called the Prospector that has a drive system that has undergone some major design changes since the saw was first introduced in 1985; a 14-inch unit called the Lil Nugget; and an 18-inch saw called the 49er. (See Illus. 126–131.)

These saws are manufactured in the United States. All have essentially the same cast-aluminum construction and blade suspension systems. (See Illus. 127 and 128.) All of Strong's saws have a 2½-inch maximum depth of cut. The larger saws have a novel belted-drive system that provides 3 speeds: 900, 1,200, and 1,500 strokes per minute. A very small neoprene rubber belt rides in the V-grooves of the pulleys. This system appears to be very efficient and slip-free. (See Illus. 130.) The 14-inch Lil Nugget has three speeds of 1,000, 1,300, and 1,600 strokes per minute. Strong Tool Design Company is located at RR 1110, Whick, Kentucky 41390.

The Scrollmate parallel-arm scroll saw is a new product distributed by Sakura, U.S.A., 360 South Monroe St., Xenia, Ohio 45385. This saw has a 14-inch throat, a belted-drive system that provides speeds of 1,050, 1,361, and 1,750 strokes per minute, a 2-inch maximum cutting depth, a 1-inch stroke, and a basically all-cast aluminum construction. This saw is designed essentially like the Strong's 14-inch saw described above. In fact, Sakura purchased the rights to the basic design from Strong Tool Design Company in 1988. The saw is manufactured abroad, where it is painted another color, and undergoes some minor changes.

The Fretmaster scroll saw (Illus. 135–137) is a relatively new saw developed and sold by Reidle Products, Box 58, Yuba, Wisconsin 54634. This scroll saw, available in kit form or assembled, is designed especially for fretwork, as its name implies. The Fretmaster combines many advantageous features from the old foot-powered saws with some new and innovative features. If you will be working with lighter materials and making very delicate cuts, this saw is worth looking at.

The best features of the Fretmaster are its slower cutting speed and its blade holder, with which you can thread the blade easily to make interior cutouts. (See Illus. 137.) The top and lower blade holders are essentially

Illus. 126. Strong Tool Design's 18-inch "49er" saw.

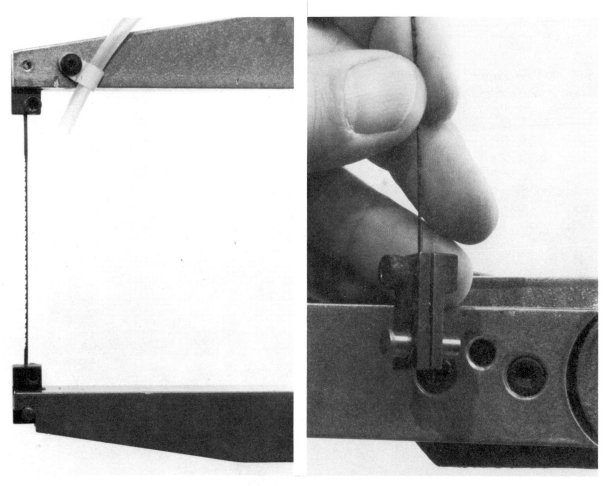

Illus. 127 (above left). The blade-suspension system on the 49er saw. Only the lower blade clamp is removable. Illus. 128 (above right). A special hole in the hold-down arm secures the lower blade clamp during blade installation. The teeth must point downward and face towards the rear of the machine.

Illus. 129. A closer look at some of the structural features on the Strong scroll saw. Note the three-speed step pulleys, the pitman connected to the lower arm, and the bellows for the sawdust blower line.

Illus. 130. A look at the underside of the "49er" 's base. Note the aluminum cast rib construction, the V-grooved motor pulley, and the unique round, elastic neoprene drive belt that just ⅛ inch in diameter.

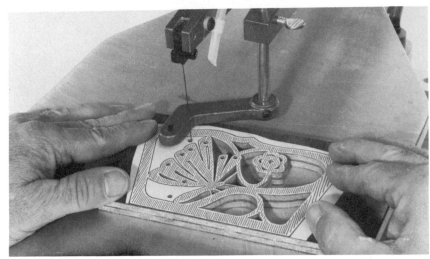

Illus. 131. The operator's view on the Strong 49er saw. Note the hold-down and dust-blower tube attached to the saw arm.

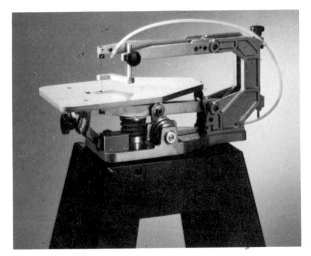

Illus. 132 (above left). The Sakura 14-inch three-speed belted-drive scroll saw. Illus. 133 (above right). The round belt and step pulleys on the Scrollmate scroll saw make it easier for the operator to change speeds on the saw because he doesn't have to loosen motors or pulleys.

(Left) This solid walnut Eiffel Tower, ¼ and ³⁄₁₆ inch thick and 36 inches high, was made by James Reidle. It has a clear Deft finish. (Above) This close-up reveals the details on the lower portion of the Eiffel Tower. This project demonstrates the importance of maintaining continuity when sawing straight and curved lines.

A

This dragon was made from ¼-inch-thick oak by John Polhemus.

This combination wall shelf and cabinet was made by Carl Weckhorst.

B

Overlaid Victorian-style letters applied to a sign board and small box.

These miscellaneous fret cuttings were made by the "fretworker" Kirk Ratajesak.

(Right) This large clock was made from 5/16-inch-thick butternut by James Reidle, Sr. in the 1940s on a foot-powered scroll saw. It stands 50 inches high. (Below left) A small wall clock of solid oak. (Below center) Cathedral clock made by Carl Weckhorst. (Below right) German-style clock made of 3/8-inch-thick solid pine.

D

(Above) Miniature wall clock by Kirk Ratajesak. Compare the size of this unusual piece to the pencil in the photograph. (Top left, center, and below) Miniature furniture by Kirk Ratajesak.

E

(Above left) A small table by Carl Weckhorst. (Above right) This wall clock by Carl Weckhorst is 29 inches long. (Right) This interesting lampshade, by Carl Weckhorst, was assembled with shop-made corner mouldings.

F

(Left) A fret-sawn bird cage by Carl Weckhorst. (Below left) Wall candle holders by Carl Weckhorst. (Below right) This ornate jewelry box was made entirely of thin stock by Carl Weckhorst.

G

This Lord's Prayer plaque, made by Carl Weckhorst, measures 30 × 35 inches.

H

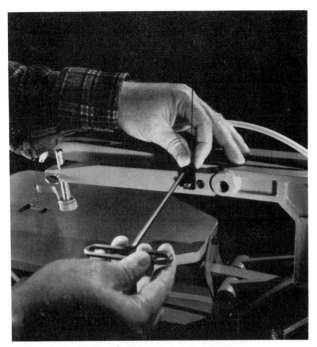

Illus. 134 (above left). A blade changer located on the hold-down arm on the Scrollmate scroll saw secures the lower removable lower blade clamp as it is secured to the bottom end of the blade with an allen wrench. The upper blade clamp is fixed in the arm and cannot be removed. Illus. 135 (above right). The Fretmaster scroll saw, developed and sold by Reidle Products, Box 58, Yuba, Wisconsin 54634, is available either in kit form or assembled.

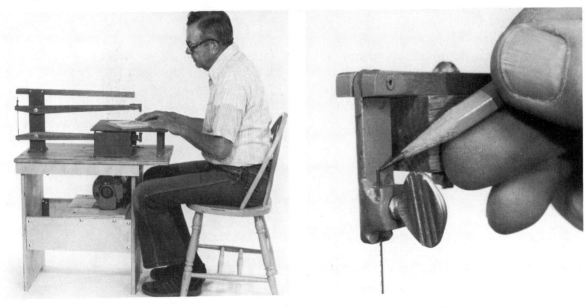

Illus. 136 (above left). Fretmaster scroll saws are designed to accommodate a comfortable regular chair-height sawing position. Illus. 137 (above left). The blade on a Fretmaster saw can be threaded quickly because of the saw's wooden arms and this simple but efficient blade-clamping system that utilizes just a thumbscrew. The blade is inserted into the holder at approximately the same height every time, and there is no need to adjust blade tension.

identical. To quickly thread the blade, simply do the following: Press down on the upper wooden arm while loosening the thumbscrew, thus releasing the blade; thread the blade through the work; again press down on the arm as you retighten the blade in its holder with the thumbscrew; and continue to saw. The manufacturer claims that its saw is the quickest blade-threading scroll saw ever made. This claim seems to be well substantiated.

The Fretmaster uses 5-inch plain-end blades, so it can cut the very smallest of inside openings. The blade can be tensioned with the compression spring at the rear. Once you have set the tension, it needs no further attention, even when you thread or change blades.

The saw has a 1¼-inch stroke that carries the sawdust well out of the cut. It has an 18-inch throat capacity and cuts at the rate of 575 strokes per minute. This rate is slower than usual, but it is, in fact, a perfect rate for precision cutting and for controlling the saw. The table is fixed and provides no provision for tilting or bevel-sawing work. Its table has a small hole for the blade, thus providing support near the blade; this is important when you are cutting fragile work.

The Fretmaster has two design features that all scroll saws should have: First, the saw is designed for a sitting, chair-height operation, which you will find more comfortable when working at the saw for extensive periods of time. (See Illus. 136.) Secondly, this saw has an extra overarm to which you can attach a task light (Illus. 138) and/or clamp several other devices such as a vacuum or a dust-blower attachment. (See Illus. 139–141.)

Though the Delta 18-inch variable speed scroll saw is described and illustrated in the *Scroll Saw Handbook*, it should also be mentioned here. It has two features conducive to fretwork: a variable-speed system and an up-front blade tensioning system. This variable-speed feature, like those on other saws, is helpful for beginners, who should cut at slow speeds, and for those sawing thin materials, during which a slower cutting speed is almost essential.

Some saws do not come with a sawdust blower; others come with blowers that are not very effective. Zach Etheridge has conceived of an idea in which you can add your own system by simply using a tiny aquarium air pump. (See Illus. 144–146.) This air pump will provide just the right amount of air flow for almost all sawing jobs. One advantage of this system is that you can bend the copper tubing so that all sawdust can be directed *away* from the operator.

The air flow on almost all saws is directed right at the operator. This air-borne dust is unsafe to breathe and should be avoided.

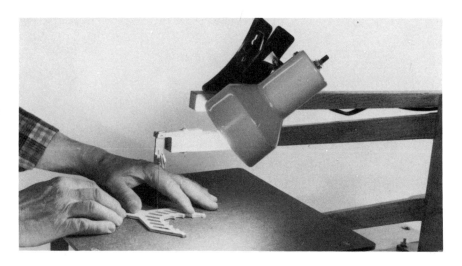

Illus. 138. Good lighting is always important in all fine scroll sawing. Here, clamp-on task lighting is supported by the extra arm on the Fretmaster saw.

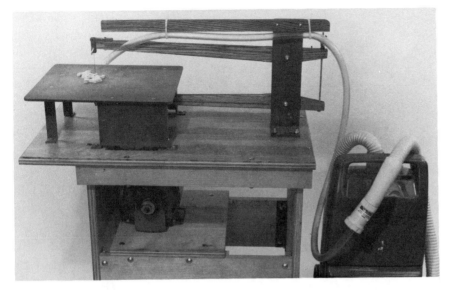

Illus. 139. Here the home vacuum linked to a plastic hose draws away fine airborne particles.

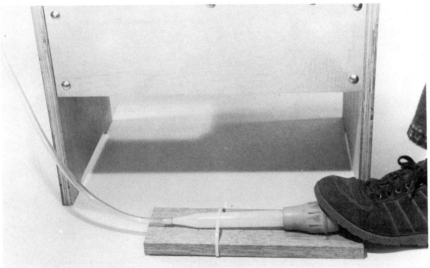

Illus. 140. This foot-operated cook's baster sends air to the cutting area via a plastic hose; this disperses the sawdust from the cutting line. This inexpensive system is remarkably effective and can be rigged up on almost any saw that does not have a dust blower as standard equipment.

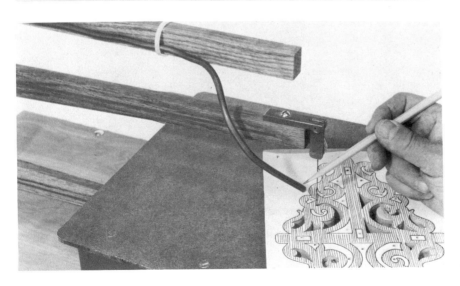

Illus. 141. Shown here is the working end of the "baster-blower"—a length of soft copper tubing that is bent to direct air to the desired area.

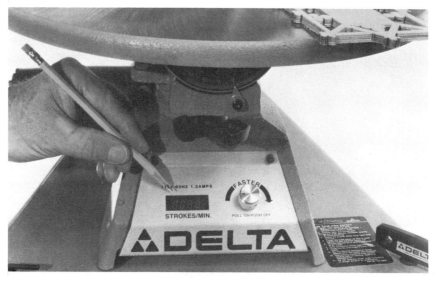

Illus. 142. The variable-speed control on the 18-inch Delta Scroll saw. Here its digital read-out shows a speed of just 80 strokes per minute. The control has a range of less than 40 to 2,000 strokes per minute.

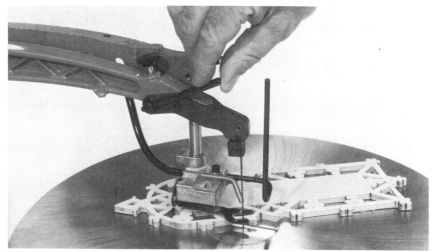

Illus. 143. One handy feature on the Delta 18-inch saw is its up-front blade tensioning. However, adjusting the hold-down, blower, and guard is rather cumbersome, and it may be better if you remove these parts when doing intensive fine fretwork in the home shop.

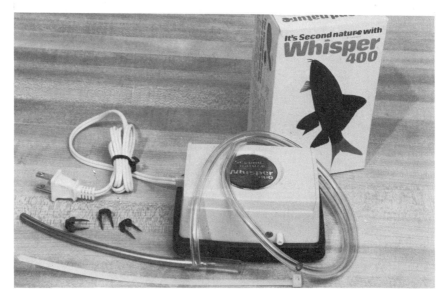

Illus. 144. To add your own sawdust blower to any saw without the accessory, you need a tiny aquarium pump and plastic and soft copper tubing.

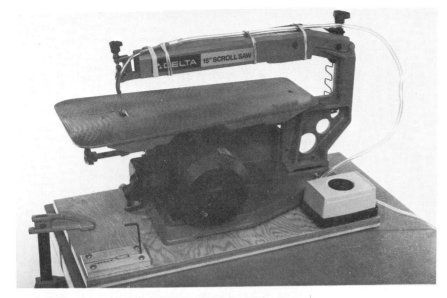

Illus. 145. Shown here is one way to add a sawdust blower to the 15-inch Delta saw and others similar in design.

Illus. 146. The air from the aquarium pump is fed into this copper tubing nozzle. Note how the copper is slightly flattened at the end and bent to deflect sawdust away from the operator. Several rubber bands stretched over the tubing hold it all in place.

Use a dust mask if you can't change the direction of air flow on your saw.

Incidentally, the homemade blower system shown in Illus. 144 and 145 will be more effective if you slightly flatten the end of the copper tubing with a pair of pliers. This channels the air so that it is aligned more directly with the line of cut. (See Illus. 146.)

If you cannot find a small aquarium pump at your local department store or pet shop, you can order the complete kit as shown in Illus. 144 from Highland Hardware, 1045 N. Highland Ave., N.E., Atlanta, Georgia 30306.

BLADES

The saw blades most widely used for hand and power fretwork are simply called scroll/ fretsaw blades. (See Illus. 147.) They are a standard 5 inches long and have plain ends. Their most common sizes, ranging from fine to coarse, are 2/0, 0, 1, 2, 3, 4, 5, 6, 7, 9, and 11. These blades generally have two basic tooth designs: a wide-spaced, or skip, single-tooth design or a wide-spaced, or skip, double-tooth design. However, there are other types of blades such as metal piercing or jewellers blades, spiral blades (which cut in all directions), scroll saw blades with regular teeth, and pin-type blades. Most power

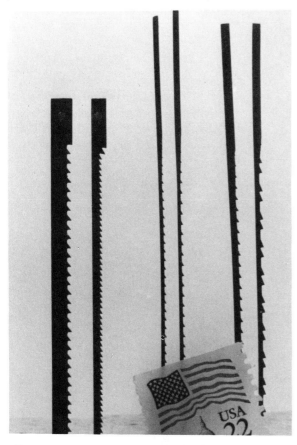

Illus. 147. Some typical saw blades. They are, as follow: at left, coarse and fine pin-end blades for use with the Dremel Power scroll saw; No. 5 and No. 7 plain-end blades; and at right, a No. 11 standard plain-end blade, and a No. 11 skip double tooth blade.

scroll saws (and hand frames) accept a 5-inch plain-end blade. Some saws such as the Dremel saw and the Sears 16-inch Craftsman scroll saw take a pin-end blade. The pin-end blade used on the Dremel saw is only 3 inches long.

Trial and error is the best way to determine which size and type of blade cuts best. A specific blade size may please one individual, but not another. Begin with a No. 5 or No. 6-size blade. As a general rule, don't use a fine blade when you can use a coarser one to obtain the desired degree of precision cutting. Coarser, heavier blades will minimize blade breakage, will not heat as quickly, and will cut faster, thus increasing production. However, for delicate work, use finer blades. You may have to experiment with different kinds of solid woods such as oak, pine, basswood, or walnut, and different plywoods such as birch, oak, or mahogany to determine which is the best blade to use in each case. You may find that a particular size blade cuts different materials satisfactorily.

The type of saw you are using, the speed of the blade, complexity of design, and the thickness of the material will determine which blades cut best. Complete information covering all aspects of blade use can be found in the *Scroll Saw Handbook*.

III
WOOD MATERIALS

It takes about the same amount of effort to find and select the proper cutting material for fretwork as it does for other woodcraft projects. Depending upon your experience, location, and other circumstances, obtaining project materials can be either a routine matter or an involved task. What should also be considered here is that there are vast differences in individual preferences regarding the specific wood species used, whether it should be left natural or stained, its hardness grade, type (solid or plywood), and much more. This is a subject far too comprehensive to be addressed adequately in this book. Instead, in this chapter we will give our opinions on the best material to use in a particular situation and how to obtain it. Also included are descriptions of the most popular woods and an examination of some of the new types of sheet materials (plywoods) that have recently become available that can be used for certain fretwork projects.

A prudent scroll sawer does not invest a lot of time and effort making an exquisite or fancy fret-cut piece using low-grade or inappropriate materials. Nor does the experienced craftsperson waste high-quality material on crude or marginal designs and utility objects. The material chosen must be appropriate for the project at hand. (See Illus. 148–152.)

Everyone knows that wood varies in range from poor quality and very inexpensive to high-grade and very expensive. It may be available locally or you may have to have it

Illus. 148. This solid-oak-wood project was made by Carl Weckhorst. Note all of the exposed edges. Imagine what this project would look like if it were made of cheap plywood.

Illus. 149. This project was cut from mahogany, which not only cuts well, but, because of its color, finishes naturally to a deep red.

Illus. 150. The project on the left was made of ¼-inch plywood, and the one on the right of ¼-inch solid wood (oak). Which looks better?

Illus. 151. Solid walnut always cuts cleanly and looks good for any project.

Illus. 152. Natural pine, a wood that has a fairly bland grain (figure) but a dainty look, is a good choice for this wall clock project. The pattern of the wood does not clash with the elegant lines of the design profile itself.

shipped from thousands of miles away. Regardless, the ultimate objective is to obtain the best material when you have determined all of your requirements. Because fretwork is so labor-intensive, try to use materials of better overall quality whenever possible. In the final analysis you'll appreciate the fact that you have used high-quality wood once you get a good look at your completed project.

SOLID WOODS

All early fretwork was made with solid wood because plywood wasn't available. Local woods were used. Softwoods were cheap, plentiful, and could be easily cut with hand or foot-powered saws. Spanish cedar wood, salvaged from cigar boxes, looked much like mahogany and was used a great deal because

it was the proper thickness, cut easily, and did not cost anything. In the 1940s beautiful thin pine boards were salvaged from wooden fruit crates that could be gotten from the local grocer for free.

Today, just about any species of solid wood is available to everyone. (See Illus. 153.) And almost any species can be used as long as it cuts satisfactorily, looks good, and is appropriate for the project(s) at hand. A softwood such as pine, for example, may make a perfectly beautiful and functional wall clock, but is not durable enough to serve as a letter opener. There are many more varieties of solid wood than plywood simply because all woods are not made into plywood. Serious fretworkers and the masters of fretwork art today prefer solid wood for three basic reasons: (1) The edges of solid wood obviously look better; (2) the parts visible from both sides can be more easily and uniformly finished; and (3) solid woods are more authentic-looking and better to use when projects are being reproduced from very old patterns and designs.

Many woodworkers now own their own band or table saw resaws and have their own equipment for reducing thick stock to thinner material. (See Illus. 154 and 155.) However, those who don't have such equipment can order wood of almost any thickness through the mail.

The following list and descriptions of various woods are not totally complete, but represents the wood species that have been used for fretwork over a period of time and/or that are available by mail order from one or more sources.

Amaranth is a very hard South American wood that's also called purpleheart because of its purple coloring. It is generally difficult to work, is expensive, and is not always readily available from conventional sources. It does make some striking ornaments, small decorative frets, and overlays.

Ash is a coarse, open-grain hardwood that is not recommended for very small ornate

73

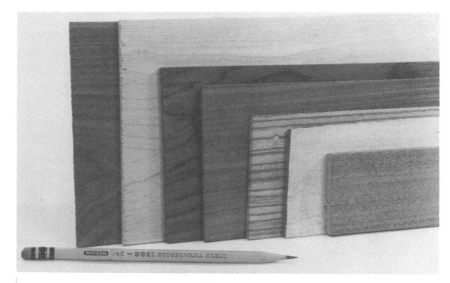

Illus. 153. Some solid hardwoods ⅛ and ¼ inch in thickness, shown from left to right, are as follow: American plain-sawn walnut and sugar maple, Brazilian rosewood, African vermilion and zebra, Canadian birds'-eye maple, and American quarter-sawn walnut.

Illus. 154. A typical home-shop planer. Machines such as this are ideal for processing your own materials, and will reduce stock to a ¼-inch thickness easily.

Illus. 155. Support any stock you are planing to less than ¼ inch in thickness on another board or plywood, as shown. Hold both pieces tightly together to start, and the machine will feed itself into the work as usual.

fretwork. It is a very strong wood with a brown heartwood (central area of the tree) and a lighter colored sapwood (between the heartwood and the bark). It should be pre-drilled for nail or screw assembly; otherwise, it will split. Ash takes almost all finishes nicely, and is a medium-priced wood.

Basswood is a fairly soft, closed-grain domestic wood that is sometimes called linden. Technically classified as a hardwood, it ranges in color from light brown to nearly white. It is a good choice for carving fret-sawn work and for making architectural frets and thicker work because it cuts cleanly and easily. As a rule, basswood is considered very inexpensive when compared to other hardwoods.

Beech is a hard, strong wood that has a tendency to warp when seasoned. It ranges in color from light brown to reddish and generally is not listed by mail-order dealers.

Birch is a hard, closed-grain wood that ranges in color from light brown to reddish and has a thick, pale sapwood. Birch is used for beautiful furniture, cabinetry, and is made into plywood. It cuts very cleanly, and the better grades of solid woods take dark stains nicely. It ranges in cost from medium to expensive.

Bubinga varies in color from pale red to deep-reddish brown and is fairly hard and heavy. It cuts cleanly, finishes nicely, and is moderately priced. It has been used primarily as quality thin veneers, but is now available as a solid wood in various thicknesses.

Butternut, when naturally finished, is a beautiful golden-brown wood with a rich grain (figure). It is a fairly soft wood that can be sawn easily if the saw has a sharp blade. It is also difficult to sand smoothly. Butternut has a color much like teak, but its grain pattern is more similar to that of walnut. In fact, some call it "white walnut." Butternut can be purchased for a reasonable amount of money, but is hard to find. Still, its worth using.

Cedar comes in many varieties and colors. Most cedar wood has a pleasing fragrance. All varieties of cedar resist decay very well and can be cut easily, which makes them ideal for thicker, exterior architectural fretwork. White cedar generally varies in color from white to light brown. Aromatic cedar is knotty, and is often bright red with a vivid white sapwood. Western red cedar ranges in color from yellowish brown to deep reddish-brown.

Cedar generally does not warp when seasoned. It is straight-grained except where deflected by knots, moderately priced, but is not widely used for fine fretwork because it has a fragile short grain and can splinter fairly easily. Because it is soft, it takes stains poorly.

Cherry is a beautiful closed-grain hardwood. It is reddish brown in color, cuts smoothly, stains easily to darker colors, and takes all finishes very well. It is readily available and moderately priced for a fine hardwood.

Chestnut is a coarse-textured wood of a pleasing grayish-brown color. It can be cut fairly well but is not a popular wood because its supply is diminishing.

Colobolo, also called Nicaragua rosewood, is a very beautiful and very expensive wood. It is quite hard, and heavy. It is reddish with dark-brown streaks. It cuts very smoothly when sharp tools are used and can be polished beautifully.

Ebony is a very hard, dense wood that is extremely dark. It is used for occasional fine work such as jewelry making, and is used by the fretworker for inlays. It dulls tools quickly and is generally difficult to cut but can be polished very smoothly. It is also expensive. This wood is best left for woodturners and wood-carvers.

Elm—a beautiful dark brown wood that is often tinged with red—should be used more often by woodworkers and fret sawers in general. One distinct disadvantage of this wood is that it will warp when seasoned. Elm is available in hard and soft varieties and goes by many names such as "slippery" elm, "basket" elm, etc. It generally ranges in cost from inexpensive to moderately priced.

Fir (Douglas and white) has large prominent growth rings. It is made into construction plywood with coarse- and wild-grain figures. Generally, fir, like some cedars, should not be used for fine work because it splinters easily and does not take a finish well. Use fir for economical utility-type projects or for outside painted signs if you have sawn them from exterior-grade plywood.

Holly, often called white holly or boxwood, is an all-white (heartwood and sapwood) species that is uniform and compact in texture. It can be sawn easily, even though it is heavy and hard. This wood is excellent to use for small contrasting inlays and overlays, but should not be used for large pieces. Lower grades of holly have bluish-green streaks.

Jelutong is a very light wood that ranges in color from white to buff. Grown in Malaya, its heartwood and sapwood are very uniform throughout in texture and color. Jelutong has recently become a favorite of professional wood-carvers and is excellent for thicker fretwork. It looks best with a natural finish or left unfinished. Jelutong is fairly expensive and difficult to obtain.

Koa is a wood native to the Hawaiian Islands. It has a beautiful figure and comes in a wide variety of rich brown shades. It works well and can be finished beautifully. It varies in price from expensive to very expensive.

Lacewood, also known as silky oak, is popular in Australia and Europe, where it is grown. It varies in color from soft pink to reddish brown. Its very distinctive figure is lace-like in design because of the arrangement of highly visible, large dark-brown flecks; because of this design, lacewood does not look attractive when used for delicate fretwork.

Lauan looks like grayish-pink mahogany. It is a very coarse-textured, open-grained wood that has weak fibres, and is used principally as inexpensive plywood and as sheet underlayments. It is usually associated with lower-quality wood products and therefore is not recommended for fine work other than that used as supportive backing when you are sawing out other thin or delicate work.

Mahogany comes in many varieties. African, Honduras, and Philippine mahogany are the most popular. All mahoganies are generally similar in grain and texture, and they range in color from pale to deep red. Mahogany has excellent sawing qualities and takes penetrating oil finishes beautifully. Prices vary from medium to very high, depending upon the type of mahogany used.

Maple also comes in many hard and soft varieties. Maple sapwood varies in color from soft brown to yellow to almost white. Hard or sugar maple is heavy and uniformly fine-textured. Maple cuts cleanly and smoothly, when good tools are used, and it takes all natural finishes beautifully. Curly or "bird's-eye" maple is the most expensive. It has numerous small knots, each simulating the look of a bird's eyes. Maple is widely used by woodcrafters, and is excellent for certain fretted projects. Plain maple is reasonably priced and readily available.

Oak is a well-known wood that comes in many varieties. Red oak is the most well-known and abundant type of oak. The wood is heavy, porous and quite hard. It cuts very cleanly with sharp tools, and takes natural finishes or oil stains beautifully. Because of its reasonable price, it is popular for all woodcrafts, including fretwork.

Padouk (sometimes called vermilion) is an exceptionally rich looking wood with a very deep-red color. Generally, this hard wood has good overall working characteristics and looks great when oil-finished. It is reasonably priced when compared to other imported woods.

There is a great variety of *pine* wood. Some types are far more desirable than others. White and sugar pine are the best for woodcrafts; other cheaper varieties are often loaded with pitch, which makes sawing and finishing difficult. Pine is ideal for large projects and architectural fretwork. Because it is economical and can be cut easily with almost all scroll saws, it is a good choice for young-sters and beginners. As a rule, pine is dif-ficult to stain evenly, so it is best finished natural.

Poplar is also called yellow poplar because it ranges in color from cream to yellow green-ish. Poplar cuts very easily because it is a fairly light softwood, is straight grained, and has a uniform texture. It requires very careful finishing. Though it is inexpensive and often used for scroll sawing, be selective when using it in fine fretwork. Make sure that the wood is in keeping with the spirit of the de-sign.

Redwood is a soft, uniformly textured straight-grained wood that cuts very smoothly. It is a good, reasonably priced choice for thick fretwork and painted exte-rior, architectural work. It's similar in color to cherry or mahogany, but is not an appropri-ate substitute for those fine hardwoods.

Rosewood is one of the best, but one of the most expensive, woods for fret cutting. It is very hard, oily, and very often gummy, but it cuts easily in thinner dimensions. Rosewood has an elegant reddish-brown color and looks best with a natural oil finish.

Teak has a rich-golden brown color that makes it a favorite of many woodcrafters, but it is expensive. It is a hard wood that can be cut fairly well, and looks best with a natural oil finish.

Walnut is very dark brown in color and is sometimes called "black walnut." It is per-haps the best of all woods for all elegant or delicate fretwork projects. It is of medium density, saws easily, and looks superb with a natural Danish oil finish. Walnut is moder-ately expensive, but for certain projects it can almost be considered the only choice.

Willow is a grayish-brown wood that is lightweight and fairly soft. You will have to use sharp saw blades on willow to cut its weak fibres cleanly. Because it is inexpensive and has an interesting color, it may be worth-while for you to try a small quantity of the wood to determine if you like it. Some wood-workers praise it, and others condemn it.

Zebrawood is an African wood so named because the deep brown-striped figure on the lighter-brown surface resembles the stripes on a zebra. The bark from the tree can be as much as one foot thick. This is an ex-pensive hardwood that is very striking in ap-pearance, and which can be cut and finished well. However, it may not look attractive when it is used for certain fine fretwork. Some fretworkers may find a suitable pur-pose for zebrawood.

Thin, Warped Wood

You may find that some of your thin, solid wood has warped while in storage or has ar-rived in a mail-order shipment warped. Thin wood, as a rule, has a high tendency to cup. (See Illus. 156.) This is especially true of thin boards that are plain- (or flat-) sawn from the tree. Quarter-sawn boards do not cup nearly as much. (See Illus. 157.)

Cupping is a curved distortion across the width of a board. A curved bending that oc-curs lengthwise is referred to as bowing. Cupping and bowing can be corrected fairly easily and quickly if the stock is ¼ inch or less in thickness. Slightly dampen the concave side of the board with a moist rag or a vapor-izer spray like those used in Windex or liquid cleaner bottles. Then carefully apply heat to the convex (opposite) side of the board. Use a flameless heat source such as a hair dryer or an electric hot plate.

Once you have fret-cut or sawn out the wood, warpage is not usually a serious prob-lem because the openings made in the stock relieve those stresses that induced the wood to warp in the first place. Good finishing practices also help to minimize warpage.

PLYWOODS

Today, plywood in one form or another is widely used for fretwork. (See Illus. 158.) In spite of the fact that plywood has unsightly edges, it offers many advantages. Quality plywood is consistently uniform in thick-

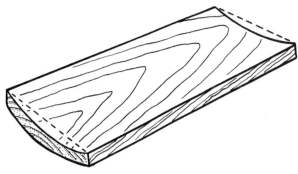

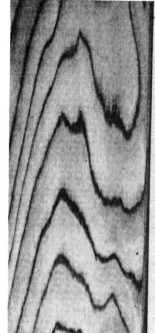

Illus. 156 (above left). A flat, plain-sawn board that has "cupped." To remove the cupped distortion, slightly dampen the top of the board and apply a flameless heat source to the bottom surface. Illus. 157 (right). The grain pattern on the face of a board identifies how it was cut from the tree. At left is a plain-sawed board; compare it with the straight lines of the quarter-sawed board on the right.

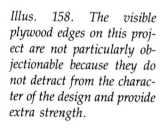

Illus. 158. The visible plywood edges on this project are not particularly objectionable because they do not detract from the character of the design and provide extra strength.

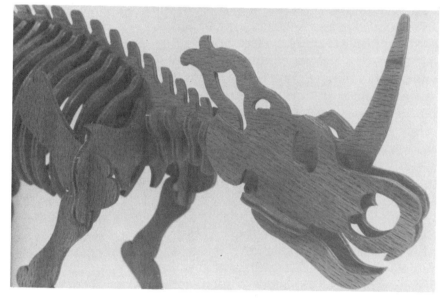

ness, does not warp as much as solidwood, and is stronger, which is an advantage when it is used for extremely fragile and delicate cuttings. One of plywood's major advantages is that it is ideal for large projects that are excessively wide. Large, thin, one-piece widths of solid wood are not commonly available, and would not be recommended for such jobs if they were.

Available are different species of plywoods

of various thicknesses that are ideal for fretwork. (See Illus. 159 and 160.) You can easily obtain birch and oak species of cabinet-and furniture-grade hardwood plywood from most building supply centers. Other good species including mahogany, cherry, walnut, teak, pine, and basswood, are available, but usually only through the more specialized suppliers.

Local building centers also offer inexpen-

Illus. 159. Shown here are three-ply ¼-inch hardwood veneer plywoods. They are, from left to right: Walnut, birch, cherry, oak, and teak. (Photo from Scroll Saw Puzzle Patterns, *by Patrick and Patricia Spielman, Sterling Publishing Co., New York)*

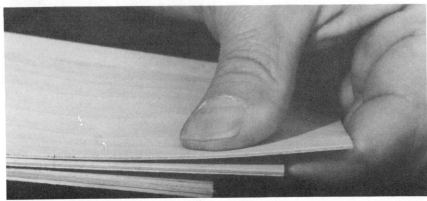

Illus. 160. These extremely thin three-ply Finland birch plywoods are ¹⁄₃₂, ¹⁄₁₆, and ⅛ inch thick. This material is idea for many projects such as ornaments, models, miniatures, silhouettes, overlays, and is a perfect way to increase output when stack cutting Luan plywood.

sive home panelling material and cheap utility plywood. Avoid fir, Southern pine and lauan construction plywood because they splinter easily and do not take a good finish. (See Illus. 161.) Specialized dealers will often offer "door skins," thin veneer plywoods used for flush door surfaces, for very reasonable prices. Some home wall panelling may prove to be a suitable and economic choice for one-sided projects such as certain wall shelves, plaques etc. In fact, sometimes these cheap wall panellings have some nice suitable hardwood veneer backs that are sound and unfinished.

Most hardwood plywood available in the United States has only one good face side and a completely different low-quality species of wood for the backers. Hardwood plywood that has two good sides is extremely expensive.

In recent years, imported Baltic birch plywood and Finland birch (called Finnish birch) plywood have become popular among United States woodcrafters. This plywood is stronger and is made with more layers (plies) of veneer per a given thickness than most of the United States-made hardwood cabinet and furniture plywood. (See Illus. 162.)

Baltic and Finland birch plywood that is less than ¼-inch is especially popular among scroll sawers. Thicker sizes, however, tend to dull scroll-saw blades more quickly because the plywood already has so many more layers of glue. For example, Finland birch that is 1⅛ inch thick has 22 plies, and Finland birch ½ inch thick has 9 plies. Most ¾-inch-thick American hardwood plywood has only 5 or 7 plies.

Baltic birch is available in thicknesses of 3 mm (⅛ inch), 4 mm (⁵⁄₃₂ inch), 5 mm (³⁄₁₆ inch), 6 mm (¼ inch), and on up to 1½ inches. Finland birch is available in thicknesses from ⅛ to 1⅛ inches. A special premium-grade plywood called aircraft plywood is also available in a Finnish birch species in thicknesses that range from ¼ inch down to a mere ¹⁄₁₆ inch (which has a remarkable 3-ply construction). (See Illus. 160.) Serious fretworkers are finding many uses for this very thin plywood, even the plywood that's only ¹⁄₃₂ and ¹⁄₁₆ inch thick. With this material you can, for example, stack together and cut at once many more layers to produce more pieces in a given time.

An imported species of plywood, jelutong, is now available from some suppliers in thicknesses that range from ⅛ to ¾ inch. It is a smooth, soft plywood that is very easy to work with. Although fretwork is seldom painted, jelutong looks attractive when painted.

Illus. 161 (above left). This project has an underlayment of ¼-inch plywood. Though inexpensive, uniform, and free from voids, this soft, open-grain material leaves ragged edges because fibres on the surface of the exit side (as shown on the right) are torn rather than are cut and severed cleanly with the saw. Illus. 162 (above right). On the left is the edge of five-ply Baltic birch; compare it to the typical ¼-inch three-ply hardwood on the right.

IV
PATTERNS

Once you have selected the wood, you are ready to use one of several methods to transfer the lines of the pattern to the wood so that the project profiles can be sawn out. However, before exploring these methods, let's examine some different types of commercially available patterns, methods of enlarging patterns, and basic ideas for actually designing your own fretwork projects.

SOURCES AND TYPES OF PATTERNS

In recent years, an increasing number of scroll saw and fretwork patterns have become available. Some of these patterns are very good and have great designs, smoothly and crisply drawn lines and are well-detailed overall. Others are poorly designed, have thick, shaky lines, and are often poorly reproduced.

The easiest patterns to use are those that come already printed full size in sheet or book form. (See *Scroll Saw Pattern Book* and *Scroll Saw Fretwork Patterns*, both by Sterling Publishing Co.) Full-size patterns are drawn or printed in different ways. Usually the full outline profiles of very old patterns and those of foreign origins will be printed in solid black or deep blue. (See Illus. 163.) Some patterns are just single-line drawings. (See Illus. 164.) Shaded single-line drawings are particularly helpful. (See Illus. 165.) Solid or filled-in patterns of highly detailed or more complex projects can cause eyestrain and irritate the fretworker because the dark

Illus. 163. Some imported fretwork patterns available from Reidle Products. Note the arrows printed on the left plan; they indicate the best grain direction.

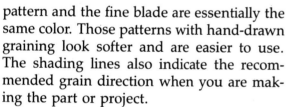

Illus. 164 (left). A typical single-line pattern from the Scroll Saw Pattern Book. *Illus. 165 (above). A typical shaded pattern, from* Scroll Saw Fretwork Patterns.

pattern and the fine blade are essentially the same color. Those patterns with hand-drawn graining look softer and are easier to use. The shading lines also indicate the recommended grain direction when you are making the part or project.

Some solid and single-line patterns have arrows printed directly on or near the pattern to indicate the most appropriate grain direction. As a general rule, the grain should run vertically in the design, or run with the longest dimension of the part or project. A pattern for a 1 × 10-inch letter opener, for example, that is made with the grain running across its width, rather than with its length, would present a serious "short-grain" problem. Thus, not only would the project turn out to be unnecessarily fragile, it would also be unattractive.

Not all project plans come full size. Those that are not full size, more often have to be enlarged to their original sizes than reduced.

There are many ways to enlarge designs. Two well-known methods of enlargement are with a pantograph or with a squared-grid system. These methods have been explored in scores of woodworking books. If you want to learn more about them, refer to the *Scroll Saw Handbook*, by Sterling Publishing Co.

The easiest way to make enlargements and one:to:one copies is with an office Xerox machine, which is probably the greatest aid for woodworkers since the invention of the saw. (See Illus. 166.) Some copy machines can also reverse or flop the pattern. This is the ability, for example, to convert a right-hand pattern into a left-hand copy. First, the original is copied onto a clear transparent piece of thin plastic. Next, this piece of thin plastic is placed on the machine and a paper copy is made of the inverted plastic. The machine produces a paper copy that is a flopped or reverse image of the first original. Overhead projection transparencies are the type of plastic used by the authors.

Illus. 166. Office copy machines with reducing and enlarging capabilities are a tremendous help for today's fretworker.

Templates

Templates are very useful full-size, thin cutouts that you can trace around to draw the design of a particular pattern directly onto the surface of the wood. (See Illus. 167.) They are basically full-sized patterns that are cut out of a stiff, rigid material.

Templates can be made from a variety of different materials. Suitable materials include tagboard, cardboard, hardboard, file folder stock, oiled stencil board, thin plastic, and the thin (⅟₃₂, ⅟₁₆, or ⅛-inch) plywood discussed in Chapter III. Some templates may be cut with a pair of scissors or a knife. The easiest way to make templates, though, is to

Illus. 167. Good templates can be easily traced.

saw them out when you cut out the project. (See Illus. 168 and 169.) However, remember that any inaccurate cuts made in the sawing will automatically be revealed each time the template is used.

Ready-cut plastic templates of various designs are now being offered to the scroll-sawing public. The most popular templates available are letter templates that come in various styles and sizes. However, also available are thin plastic templates of fretted Victorian arches, shelf brackets, miscellaneous silhouettes, and country cutouts.

Templates are more durable than paper patterns. Good templates can be used again and again. One detail should be addressed concerning self-made templates with symmetrical designs. In theory, if this pattern were to be split in two or folded vertically both halves would supposedly be exactly identical. In practice, it is best to only trace one half of the template and then flip it over on a vertical axis or centerline to draw the second half. This way, the left and right halves will be laid out and drawn precisely the same, since they were each traced from the same part of the template pattern.

Some patterns, like the one shown in Illus. 171, are only half patterns. You must flip this pattern on its centerline to complete the layout. Some patterns are quarter patterns, so you have to make four copies or trace one pattern four times to complete the full pattern. (See Illus. 172.)

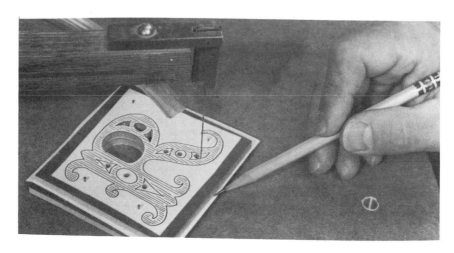

Illus. 168. A piece of stiff tagboard inserted between two pieces of wood (tacked together) and cut will simultaneously produce a reusable template as the original pattern pieces are sawn.

Illus. 169. Here is the finished template.

Illus. 170 (right). Here is a fairly detailed template of a symmetrical design that was cut (sawn) simultaneously with a wooden part. The template preserves the pattern profile so that it can be reused. Illus. 171 (far right). Some patterns, such as this one for a picture frame (reprinted from the Scroll Saw Pattern Book), are only ½ patterns and must be flipped on their center lines when you want to complete the layout.

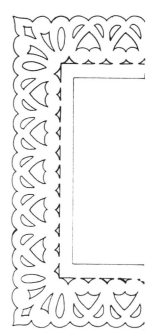

Illus. 172. Some patterns may be just ½ or ¼ of the complete project. This quarter pattern had to be copied four times. Each copy must be bonded to the surface so that the chess/checker board project can be sawed out completely.

Stencils

Stencils are templates that can be used to make patterns for either cutout pieces or cutout openings that are pierced through a solid background. (See Illus. 173–175.)

Circles and Ovals

In order to cut circles and ovals that have continuous smooth-flowing curves, it is imperative that you lay out the line(s) you will follow with the saw as perfectly as possible. Circles and ovals are the most difficult forms to cut precisely. Yet, circles and ovals are important and frequent forms for many fretwork objects, including picture frames, hand mirrors, signs, plaques, and silhouettes. Lay circles out directly onto the wood with a compass in a sharp, crisp line. Ovals, on the other hand, are more complex to draw and are harder to lay out. Do not draw any part of a true oval with a compass—even though some drafting textbooks offer a technique known as the "approximate four-center ellipse."

You can draw a true oval, or perfect ellipse, by following the easy steps demonstrated in Illus. 176–180. Although these illustrations do show a compass being used, it is used only to set off distances (as one would use a divider or ruler). It is not used to draw any part of the line that comprises the profile of the ellipse.

Some common oval sizes that are good for picture frames, mirrors, and similar projects are as follows: 2 × 3, 3 × 5, 5 × 7, 8 × 10, and 11 × 14.

Illus. 173. Stencil-type templates are helpful for designing wood signs.

Illus. 174. One way to make great signs of almost any size is to enlarge business cards and modify the letters to a stencil-style.

Illus. 175. The pattern for this sign, which measures about two feet in overall length, was enlarged from a small business card. This technique will prove helpful if you want to make custom-built signs.

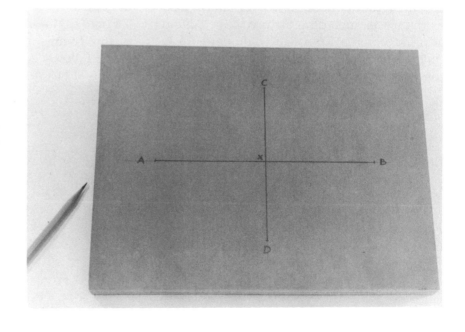

Illus. 176. The first step in laying out a true ellipse or oval. A-B equals the major diameter; C-D equals the minor diameter, which bisects and is laid out perpendicular to A-B at X.

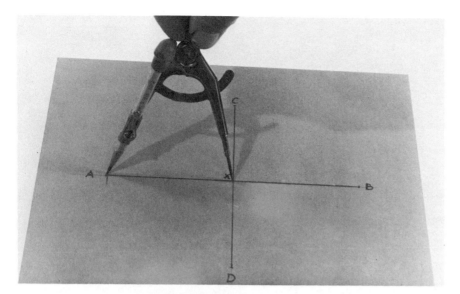

Illus. 177. Step two. Set a divider (or compass) to half the major diameter, as shown.

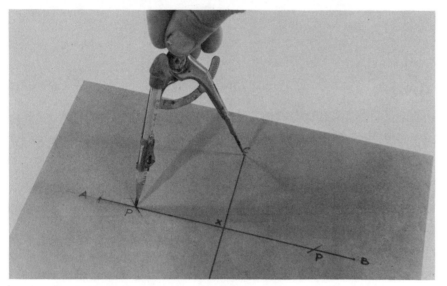

Illus. 178. Step three. With C as the base (center) point, set off P-P on line A-B. C-P is equal to A-X (that is, it is ½ the distance of the major diameter).

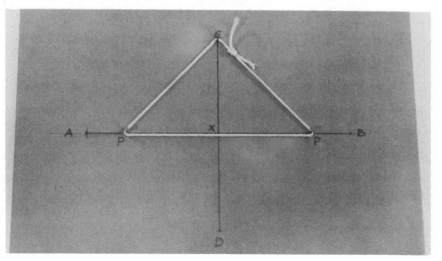

Illus. 179. Step four. Set nails, tacks, or pins at P-P and point C. Pull a string tightly around these three points and tie it securely. Remove the pin or tack at point C.

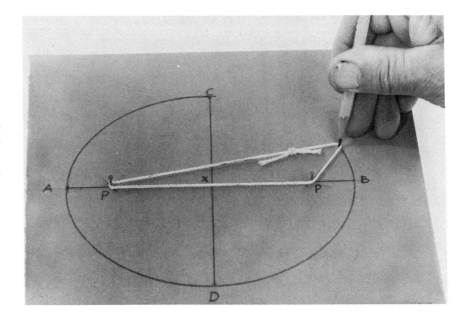

Illus. 180. Step five. Keep the string as taut as possible with a pencil, as shown, and, while simultaneously moving the pencil around, draw a perfectly true oval.

DESIGNING FRETWORK

It takes a certain amount of artistic talent to design fretwork. Included here are just a few fundamental techniques for those who might want to design fretwork patterns themselves and some basic guidelines to help the fret sawer recognize well-designed patterns and fretwork.

Start a design idea by sketching simple, single-line geometric forms, such as the outline of a heart. (See Illus. 181–183.) Illus. 184 shows one technique for designing frets that consist of ogee lines or S swirls that are typically found on French curves. Another basic method that allows you to transform one design into a series of projects or to create larger designs is using a single pattern back to back or side by side. (See Illus. 185.) You can reduce basic, familiar profile shapes to their simplest forms, and then embellish them by tactfully creating internal openings. Illus. 186 shows how a simple silhouette of a swan can provide the inspiration for a stylized version. The same principle applies when you use a stencil template, which is nothing more than a simple shape frag-

mented into pierced, open spaces. (See Illus. 187.)

Very ornate designs involving foliage, stems with veined leaves, and flowers demand a higher level of artistic talent. Observe and study actual flowers, leaves, etc., to draw the designs as accurately as possible. It would also help if you analyze the designs of the fretwork pieces shown throughout this book. You will notice that through careful observation that larger pieces are made when certain key elements, lines, and forms are repeated over and over. Also, don't forget to use an enlarging and reducing copy machine when creating your own designs.

Ties

Fretwork is more often intended to be ornamental than functional, but this does not mean that it must be fragile. Designers often incorporate certain techniques into their pieces to strengthen otherwise highly delicate frets. One method is to simply surround the design on one or all edges with a frame composed of straight or appropriately curved lines.

Wherever the design touches the border or

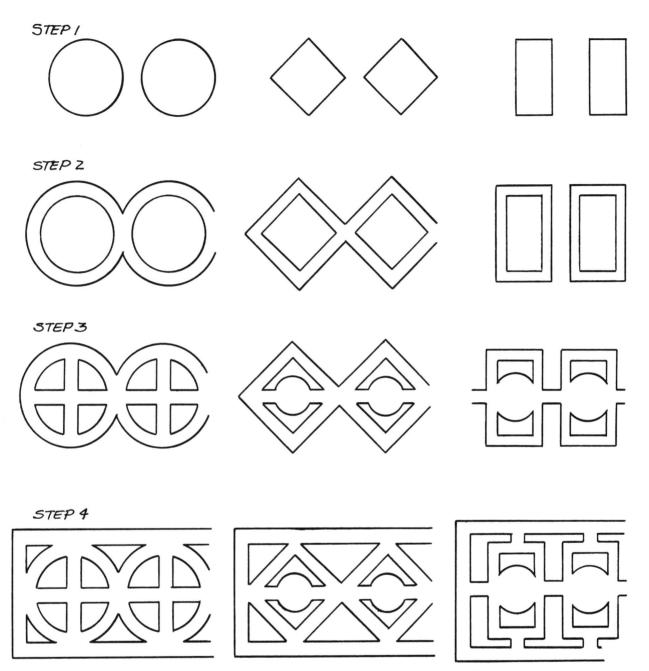

Illus. 181. One technique for developing fretwork designs is to progress from single-line geometric forms to double lines to an inserted profile. You can expand on this idea by repeating or continuing the design side by side indefinitely.

Illus. 182 (above). The basic, familiar shapes shown at the top of this drawing can be transformed to simple double-line forms, shown below, which creates interesting open spaces. Illus. 183 (right). You can further divide spaces to create new fretting or establish whatever degree of detail or design complexity you wish.

Illus. 184 (below). Using a French curve to produce a design. Step 1: A single line half pattern. Step 2: Back to back, full-pattern outline. Step 3: Double-lining interior-curved to create openings.

STEP 1   STEP 2   STEP 3

Illus. 185. One basic bracket design, shown at lower center, can be made into a number of different kinds of shelves. Note the ogee or the reversing S lines that are prominent in this design.

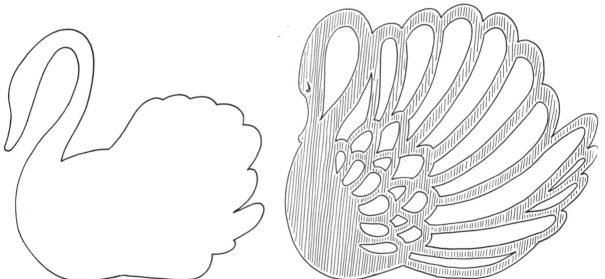

Illus. 186. Stylizing begins with a very simple profile shape that establishes just the essential realistic features. The proportions can then be stretched, reduced, or modified. You can emphasize whatever features you find most interesting. In this case, the feathering detail was developed by single line work followed with double lining, which created the open spaces.

Illus. 187. A stencil template is merely a fragmented plan of a familiar shape that provides pierced, open spaces in a solid background.

most widely used are the "tangent tie" and the "touching tie." Illus. 188 shows a tangent tie. Note that the character of the curve still remains and that the straight border line remains unbroken. In the touching tie, also shown in Illus. 188, the leaf tips touch the border naturally without distorting the leaf, giving strength as needed. It is important when you are using a tie that you do not detract from the integrity of the design. You may have to enlarge, reduce, tilt or modify the fretwork piece to ensure that the touching tie looks correct.

"Structural ties" are ties that are added to connect the design; they are an integral part of the overall ornamentation. (See Illus. 189.) The lines in "intersecting ties" cross each other and strengthen the design. (See Illus. 190.) Combining or varying these ties is an effective way to design the pattern.

Remember the following rule when designing or sawing fretwork: It's not what is to be cut away that's important, but what is to be left.

Illus. 189. Two examples of structural ties.

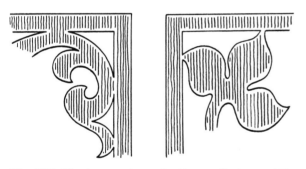

Illus 188. The two most popular ties are the tangent tie (shown at left) and the touching tie (at right).

frame, it is called a "tie." Many designs would simply fall apart without ties, which bind the design together. They also strengthen the work, and when prudently used can enhance or accentuate the look of the object.

There are various kinds of ties, but the two

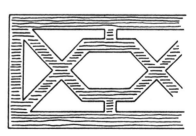

Illus. 190. When intersecting ties are used, lines are crossed to create strength in a fretted design.

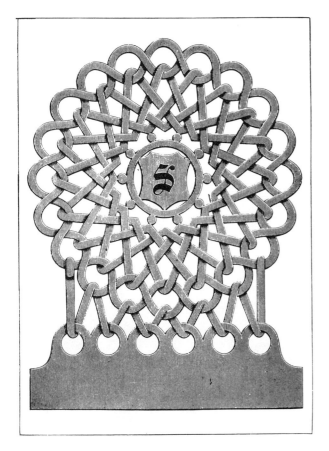

Illus. 191. You can enhance a design with some hand carving so that the lines appear to pass in and out and over and under each other. The vertical lining indicates the best grain direction; note the use of structural ties around the inside circle and the overall strength achieved by the intersecting ties, which comprise the intent of the design itself.

TRANSFERRING THE PATTERN

As you are no doubt already aware, there are various ways to get the lines of the pattern from a book or a printed sheet onto the wood for sawing. You can draw some patterns directly onto the wood as you enlarge them with graph squares. Or, if you already have a full-size template, you can simply trace around it with a soft pencil. Do not use a pen; this may smear, and will be difficult to remove later.

If you want to preserve the original paper pattern or do not want to remove pages from a book, copy the pattern with an office copier or trace over it onto thin translucent paper without marking the original. You can transfer this copy to the wood in two ways. One way is to use carbon paper and trace every line. (See Illus. 192 and 193.) This technique is more time-consuming, less accurate, and the copy is not as sharp. If you must use the pattern-tracing method, use graphite paper rather than conventional carbon paper. Carbon paper is greasy and its markings cannot be erased or sanded away easily from raw wood surfaces. Graphite paper is much easier and cleaner to use. You can also obtain white graphite paper for dark woods, which makes sawing much easier. White graphite paper or graphite paper in large sizes can probably be found at art and office supply stores.

The ideal way to handle a pattern(s) is to glue it (or a copy of it) directly onto the surface of the wood. Some woodworking books and magazine articles suggest using rubber cement, but certain spray types of adhesive are easier and faster to use. (See Illus. 194 and 195.) Two brands that are recommended are Nybco's Spra Glu and 3-M's Spray Mount Artist's Adhesive. These products are not expensive and are available in some department stores, and most art, craft, and photo shops. Some companies, including 3-M, sell spray adhesives that are intended for per-

Illus. 192. A pattern transferred onto dark wood such as walnut is more visible if white graphite paper is used.

Illus. 193. The traced pattern with carbon paper transfer (shown at left) is not as refined or as clear as the actual copy of the original pattern (shown at right) secured to the surface with a spray adhesive.

Illus. 194. Some patterns are printed with solid profiles. The pattern shown here is being cut out so that it can be bonded to the piece of wood with spray adhesive.

Illus. 195. These two spray adhesive are ideal for temporarily bonding paper patterns to wood surfaces.

manent bonding. Do *not* use these spray adhesives.

When using temporary bonding spray adhesives, spray just a little of the adhesive evenly onto the back of the pattern, as shown in Illus. 196. You quickly learn the proper amount of spray adhesive to use. Do not spray onto the raw wood. After a few seconds, press the pattern onto the wood with your hands. (See Illus. 197 and 198.) This creates a strong bond.

You can easily remove the pattern when you have completed sawing. (See Illus. 199.) In fact, the pattern can be removed so easily that if you are careful you can lift the entire pattern off and reapply it to another piece of wood. Best of all, hardly any residue is left on the wood (if any) and what does remain does not, to the best of our knowledge, affect the finishes that may be applied to the wood. These new spray adhesives have proven to be an almost indispensable tool for scroll sawers.

The way that you place the patterns on the stock and lay out the board for sawing can sometimes save valuable material and sawing time, so always use prudent judgment. The method shown in Illus. 200 is an effective one that's fairly common. The task involved sawing out two identical shelf brackets. The straight line edges were first trued, squared, and actually cut before the pattern was set down. Only one paper pattern was used because both brackets were sawn at the same time, one on top of the other. The dark line in Illus. 200 indicates the roughing cut that was necessary to separate the board into the two pieces. Illustrations 238–242 on pages 114 and 115 show how these parts are held together, cut, and finished.

Illus. 196. Spray a very light mist of adhesive to the back of the pattern. Do not spray directly onto the surface of the wood.

Illus. 197. Wait a few seconds, and then press the paper pattern onto the wood with your hands.

Illus. 198. Once you have secured the pattern to the wood, the saw threading holes (saw gates) can be drilled into it, and then the scroll saw can be used.

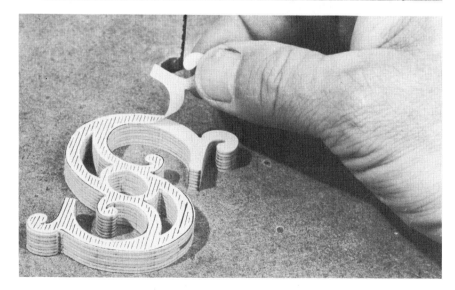

Illus. 199. After you have used the scroll saw, you can easily remove the paper patterns. The spray adhesives leave virtually no residue on the surface of the wood that could inhibit subsequent finishing.

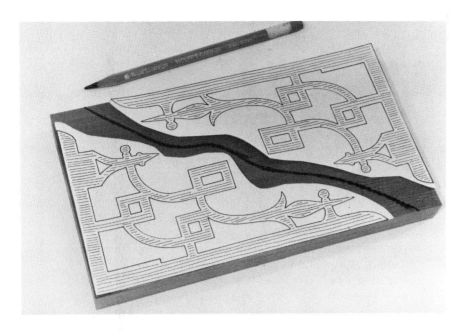

Illus. 200. Shown here is a way to conserve stock by placing patterns so that they mate each other. Note that the two outside straight edges on the pattern were previously sawn square to each other on a table saw.

V
BASIC CUTTING TECHNIQUES

This chapter presents fundamental information about the handheld fret saw frame, and also covers all of the essential principles involved in cutting fretwork with power scroll saws. Regardless of whether hand or power tools are used, many basic cutting techniques are essentially the same. Therefore, those interested in just hand work will find it helpful if they read the entire chapter.

HAND SAWING

Many woodworkers still cut fretwork by hand. (See Illus. 201.) Chapter II examines the different kinds of hand saw frames and blades available, and the wooden cutting table that is needed. Ninety-nine percent of all hand sawing is done with the blade in-

stalled in the frame so the teeth face outward and point downward towards the handle.

To correctly install a blade in the frame, clamp the lower end of the blade first. Put the upper end of the saw frame against something solid, such as a workbench edge. With your hand over the end of the handle, protecting your chest, compress the spring of the frame and secure the top end of the blade. A correctly installed blade will lay in a straight line.

Use the following procedures to thread the blade through the workpiece to make an inside cutout. Unclamp the upper end of the blade. Move the blade through the predrilled hole in the workpiece, entering the hole from the underside. Allow the workpiece to

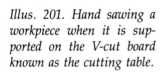

Illus. 201. Hand sawing a workpiece when it is supported on the V-cut board known as the cutting table.

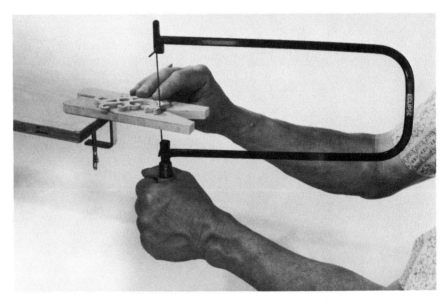

rest near the handle as you reattach the upper end of the blade to the saw frame. If necessary, use your legs to help support the workpiece during this operation.

The preferred seating position is slightly to one side of the middle of the cutting table. The starting sawing point for the workpiece is over the hole at the apex of the V-shaped aperture of the cutting board. (See Illus. 201.) Hold the workpiece down with one hand and work the saw with the other.

Keeping the saw blade vertical at all times, work the saw up and down with full, even, regular strokes. The beginner is prone to tilt the frame when rounding a corner or curve and to cut a straight line too quickly. If you allow the blade to tilt so that it is not perfectly vertical, undesirable bevel cuts will result. The pattern outline on the underside will vary from that on the upper surface. Use no or very little forward saw pressure. Fret-saw blades are designed to pull themselves into the wood.

Eye and hand coordination is essential. You have to move the workpiece to feed the cutting line to the blade while simultaneously holding the workpiece firmly to the cutting table as you saw. Use shorter strokes on tighter turns, but keep the saw moving to prevent it from binding in the cut. Continuous smooth-cutting strokes without force are essential for good sawing.

Stack sawing (also called plural cutting) oc-curs when you saw two pieces simultaneously, one on top of the other. Make this type of cut with the saw perfectly vertical if you want to produce identical pieces.

SCROLL SAWING FRETWORK

Power-driven scroll saws offer many advantages over hand saws. Speed is the primary advantage, if you have a saw with which you can quickly thread blades. Every saw should also produce perfectly true, vertical cuts all the time, every time. If yours does not, return it to the manufacturer or think about getting another one.

Safety Rules and Devices

Safety rules and suggestions are provided in almost all users' manuals, and are listed in detail in the *Scroll Saw Handbook*. Fretsawing sometimes does involve some special circumstances that may bother the safety-conscious individual(s). In fact, the very nature of the fine, open detailing of some fretwork presents some unusual sawing problems. It is often necessary to move the fingertips of one or both hands closely to each side of the blade to hold thin, delicate cuttings down on the table. (See Illus. 202.) Never place your fingers in front of or in line with the cutting path of the blade.

Hold-downs, hold-down arms, and guards are generally helpful safety devices,

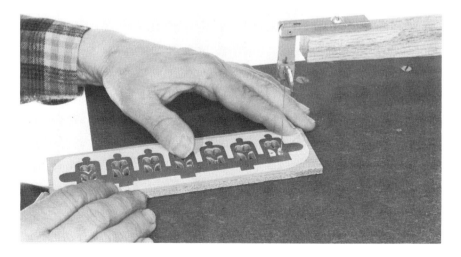

Illus. 202. Sawing without guards, hold-downs, or a dust blower requires some extra caution, but a clear, unobstructed view of the workpiece and the freedom to manipulate and control it are also important. Note how one hand to the left and close to the blade holds the work down as the other hand feeds.

but sometimes they prevent the operator from controlling the saw and, in fact, just get in the way. (See Illus. 203.) If you don't feel comfortable with these devices removed, then by all means· use them as they were intended.

One accessory that is especially helpful is a foot switch. (See Illus. 204.) A foot switch is fairly inexpensive, and is available from most saw manufacturers. It allows you to keep both hands on the workpiece without having to remove one if any trouble occurs during sawing, such as blade breakage.

When you hold the workpiece with one or both of your hands, you're always holding down the material. This is not always the case with saw hold-downs, regardless of how perfectly designed they are. A scroll saw hold-down becomes more useless the longer you continue sawing cutout openings. Much of the work that passes under the hold-down when frets are being cut already has openings cut away, and the hold-down is not effective when it's over an open space.

Good lighting is also important. It minimizes eye fatigue and promotes safe cutting. Add freestanding floodlights or spotlights if your saw is not equipped to provide adequate lighting. Two equally placed lights will eliminate disturbing shadows.

Good goggles and the proper ear protection are essential when you are using power tools for an extended period of time. So is a dust mask. Some of the most expensive and best-designed saws have the worst sawdust blowers. They may be powerful enough to get the sawdust off the layout lines, but the blower tube is angled so that the dust and air ricochets off the work, and directly to your chest or face. You won't notice this when you are sawing for a short period of time, but after cutting for approximately an hour, you'll note that the front of your shirt is covered with sawdust, and that the air-borne dust is floating right under your nose. If you do not want to wear a dust mask, modify your own blower by bending soft copper tubing so that it directs the sawdust away from you. See Illus. 144–146 for some ideas concerning various sawdust blower arrangements.

Sawing Techniques

Practice Exercises. Both hand and power tool sawers should *practice* their cuts on scrap material before starting a project. You should be able to saw a straight line, a curved line, make corners, and cut an acute angle with relative ease. Don't get discouraged if the blade seems to wander; you will eventually

Illus. 203. For this fret-sawing job, the hold-down poses two problems. First, the nail holding the two pieces together for identical cutting will strike the hold-down and inhibit feeding. Secondly, the hold-down is often useless when it passes over the openings in the workpiece that have already been cut away.

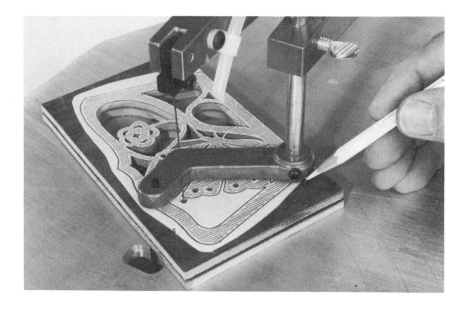

Illus. 204. A foot switch is regarded as a safety accessory because both of the operator's hands can be used to hold down and control the work. (Photo courtesy of AMI)

learn how to control it. Begin with a number 5 or 6 saw blade.

A scroll saw cuts faster across the grain than with it. Allow for this tendency when cutting circular patterns that shift rather quickly from with-the-grain cuts to cross-grain sawing. When practice cutting, you will soon develop your own way of cutting when encountering different sawing situations, and will find out what you can and cannot do with your saw.

Illus. 205 incorporates effective exercises for learning straight-line sawing and cornering techniques. Begin the first exercise by starting at point A and sawing to B. Turn the saw sharply at B with an "on-the-spot" turn while holding the workpiece firmly down. When making on-the-spot turns, it is important that you hold back on the saw while turning. Saw line C and continue to point D. The points or outside corners at D can be cut

two ways. One way is to saw slightly beyond the point and then make an on-the-spot turn, which will bring the blade into position to saw the next line. The better way, which will leave a perfectly sharp point, is shown at X. Cut past the corner (X) and make a looping turn into the waste area that will bring the blade around and in line so that you can continue cutting. (See Illus. 206.)

A third outside cornering method, which in some cases is even easier for cuts like this, is also shown in Illus. 205. Simply cut from E to F, and then back out and cut from G to F. Then continue by cutting H to I, etc., repeating as necessary. This is a cutting process in which you saw a sharp corner from two directions.

Illus. 207 shows some inside cornering techniques. Clean cornering is always essential. The errors shown in the illustration are common ones that are not considered very serious; they are, however, considered tell-tale signs of work that separates the pros from the amateurs.

Illus. 208 is another cutting exercise on which you can practice sharp (acute) angular cuts. It also provides some ideas for making repetitive outside curves. Begin at A and saw to B. Here, make an on-the-spot turn and continue sawing. Or, after cutting to the very end of the layout line at B, back up about ¼ inch and make a 180-degree on-the-spot turn while keeping the teeth in the waste area. Next, back into the cut to corner B and then proceed to saw the uncut line. Illus. 209–212 show this technique being used on an acute angle of an inside opening.

An alternative way of making the repetitive outside curve and sharp, angular cuts shown in Illus. 208 is to proceed as follows: Cut

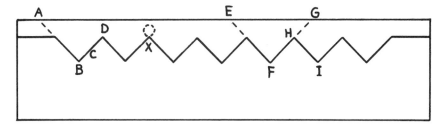

Illus. 205. A practice exercise for developing straight-line sawings and cornering techniques.

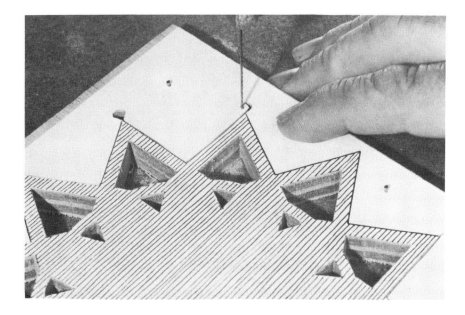

Illus. 206. To make the most accurate and the cleanest outside corner, cut it by looping around it as shown. Note the brads holding the two pieces of material together.

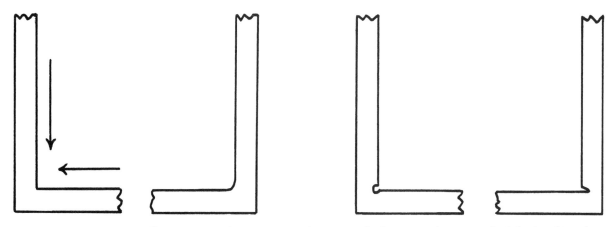

Illus. 207. Inside cornering techniques. The best one, shown on the left, is achieved by sawing from two directions or by making a sharp, 90 degree "on-the-spot" turn. All other corners show common faults.

Illus. 208. This sawing exercise will help you to make very sharp or acute angle-type cuts, such as those shown at points B, D, G.

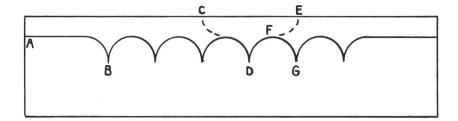

Illus. 209. The first step in cutting out an opening with a sharp (acute) angle. The cut is made from the hole and follows along one side, continuing into the corner (point).

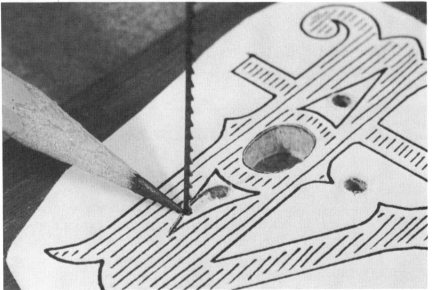

Illus. 210. Make the cut to the corner, and then "back up" the blade a short distance; here, make an "on-the-spot" 180 degree turn with the blade teeth facing inward to the waste, as shown.

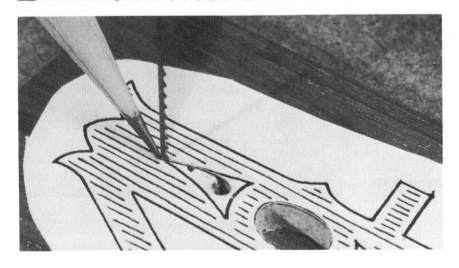

Illus. 211. Next, back the blade completely into the apex of the angle.

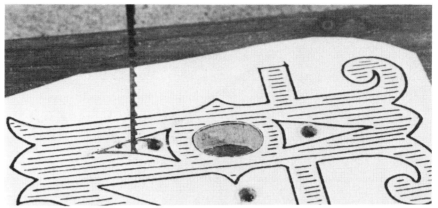

Illus. 212. Now continue the cut, sawing into the next corner.

Illus. 213. These acute angles were cut in two different ways. Both were cut with the same No. 11 blade. The cut above is the result of an "on-the-spot" turn technique that was made by sawing in, turning on the spot, and then sawing out. The cleaner cut shown below it was made by sawing both cuts inward from two directions.

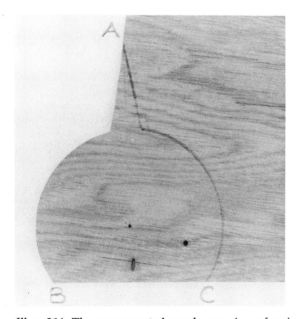

Illus. 214. The sawer must always be conscious of grain directions and the pattern being sawn. In this example, saw from A to C rather than from C to A; if you cut from C to A, you would likely break off the point before completing the entire cut.

from C to D, back out, and cut from E to D, etc. Continue cutting the other segments of the multiple curves by sawing one part of each in a direction that points from F to G. If any small "knobs" or bumps result on the curve (F) after sawing, you can remove them quickly by filing or sanding.

Drilling Blade Entry Holes. Drilling blade entry holes for interior cutouts involves more care and consideration than might be expected. First, transfer your pattern to your stock. Next, determine which areas require holes that will provide access for the blade. This blade-threading hole sometimes is also referred to as a "saw gate." The size of the bit used, the optimum location of the hole, and whether a supporting backer should be used during drilling are important considerations.

Select a bit of an appropriate size: use a ⅛- or ³⁄₁₆-inch bit for larger cutouts. If the cutout is very small, you may need a bit that is a ¹⁄₁₆ inch or smaller. With thin material, you can make a slit with a knife to separate the fibres; this slit will not be noticeable. This is an ideal technique for some veining cuts. Eventually, you will be experienced enough to determine exactly where to drill blade entry holes.

Essentially, interior spaces are composed of one of three different shapes. These shapes consist of those without points or angles, such as circles or ovals; those with corners, but not projections; and those with projecting points. The three different shapes are shown in Illus. 215. Illus. 216–218 reveal the optimum hole locations for the saw-blade starting points for each of the shapes. It's best to drill close to the point of the layout line, where you want to start cutting. This can save time and minimize the number of "knobs" or bumps that might result when sawing around to meet the point where you first started cutting.

When drilling, be aware of the possibility of "grain tear." This occasionally happens when drilling too close to the layout line. The bit grabs and tears fibres outside the hole and sometimes beyond the waste area.

At times when drilling and sawing, you will have to use backers to eliminate or minimize grain tear on the bottom or exit side of finished workpieces. Illus. 219 shows a flat scrap piece of lumber supporting the work during drilling. Holding the workpiece tightly against the backer board will greatly reduce the possibility of grain tear.

Grain tear and feathering can also occur during sawing. This is a problem that has a greater chance of occurring on certain woods. (See Illus. 220.) You can reduce splintering and grain tear if you use a finer blade and/or some inexpensive backer material such as cheap panelling or cardboard. When you are finished with the backer, it can be used as a template pattern of the sawn piece.

It is absolutely essential that there is no grain tear-out when both surfaces of the resulting part will be visible in the finished project. Extremely thin materials will require finer blades and may even require a smaller saw table opening than the one that surrounds the blade. An auxiliary saw table made of hardboard or plywood with a smaller sized hole can be secured to your existing table with double-faced tape.

Cutting Order. You must decide whether to cut out all of the inside openings first or to cut the final outside profile first. This decision depends upon the character of the pattern. Always leave the most delicate sawing for last; this will lessen the chances of accidental breakage. If there is an excessive amount of waste wood surrounding the pattern, trim it with a roughing-out cut for handling.

Usually the interior is cut first, especially if the pattern is small or the outline is elaborate and fragile. (See Illus. 221.) If the pattern is large with delicate or fragile interior cutouts,

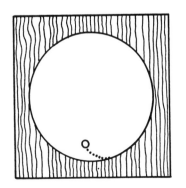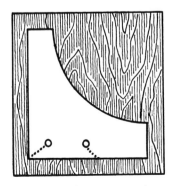

Illus. 215. *Three types of internal openings and their suggested starting hole locations. Almost all cutouts will use one of these starting hole locations.*

Illus. 216. An inside cutout that has no projection. The line should be approached abruptly, so that you will leave a small "knob" (or bump) when the cutout is completed. The knob can be worked off with the saw blade or filed clean.

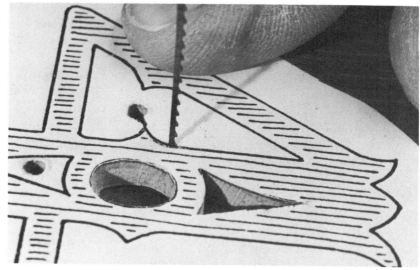

Illus. 217. A good starting point for a cutout with a sharp projection.

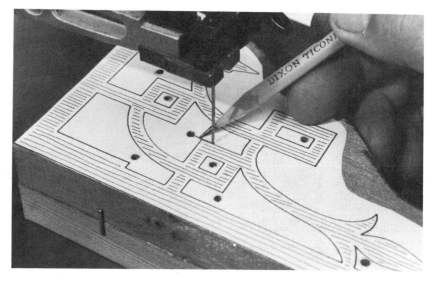

Illus. 218. Here the hole was drilled so that the cut could proceed directly to the corner and continue on the line. Note that a staple is being used to hold these two pieces together during sawing.

Illus. 219. Drilling small saw gates. The holes need to be close to the cutting lines, and it is essential that there is no grain tearing. Here the workpiece is being held tightly to a flat backer of scrap wood.

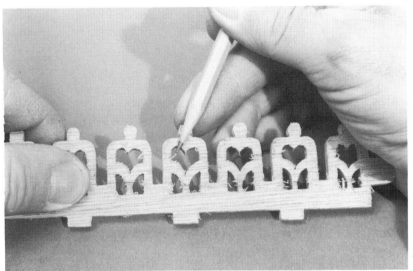

Illus. 220. This grain tearout or splintering could have been minimized if this piece was sawn while supported with a backer. The wood used for this job was a poor choice (a soft wood with a weak fibre), and the blade too coarse for this delicate pattern.

Illus. 221. Because the inside cutouts were sawn first, this work is easier to handle. Note the fragile stem, and that the staples holding the two thin pieces together for sawing are located on the outside waste areas. Note also that the blade is following the line.

then cut the outside first. Each design must be judged individually. Illus. 222–226 show a typical, basic cutting job and the essential steps involved.

Also take into consideration the order in which you will saw interior parts. If the cutting of a certain opening will leave a delicate part unprotected, then cut that opening last. (See Illus. 227.)

An extremely delicate job such as the dragon project of solid wood shown in Illus. 227 is extremely fragile and a challenging project, to say the least. It requires a fine blade, slow and careful sawing, and, if the table hole surrounding the blade is very large, a scrap plywood backer on which to support the work.

If you use the right blade, the proper material, and careful sawing techniques, you can handle the most delicate of fretted sawing jobs confident that the chances of breaking fragile parts are reduced to the very minimum.

Sawing Accurately. Sawing accuracy is achieved when you carefully follow the pattern line. You may have to correct a poorly drawn or poorly reproduced pattern before you start to saw. (See Illus. 229.) In the upper example shown in Illus. 229, the operator did not try to cut accurate straight or curved lines.

Also, the interrupted line, A to B, is not straight. "Line continuity" is a reference to the uninterrupted straightness of a line. When straight lines and long curves are broken by different types of ties, the lines really are parts of cutouts, each of which must be cut individually. This results in a number of successive shorter lines, but you must remember to focus on the integrity of the entire length. Illus. 230 depicts line continuity not only in straight and compass curved lines, but also in the irregularly curved lines of the stems. Before beginning to saw out a project, use a straight edge or a French curve to check the pattern and/or the layout lines.

Illus. 231 shows perfectly a project in which the overall visual effect of line continuity is of supreme importance.

It takes careful controlled feeding to saw straight lines, circles, and ovals, as the work is guided continuously in a straight or circular direction. Sawing out freeform leaves, for example, is much easier than cutting very specific geometrical lines. A slip or miscut on a leaf is less noticeable and easier to correct. (See Illus. 232.) Sanding and filing can correct poor sawing, but only to some extent. Do not rely on corrective measures.

Decide whether you will saw on the inside, outside, or exactly on the line, and then be consistent. Inconsistency will produce poor results and noticeable flaws in the finished project. If you are tracing or drawing

Illus. 222. Here the pattern has been applied, the saw gate holes drilled, the blade on a Fretmaster scroll saw is being threaded so that the interior openings can be cut. A number 5 blade is being used.

Illus. 223 (above left). A close look at the cutting of the inside openings. Illus. 224 (above right). After all interior cut outs have been completed, saw out the outside profile with just one continuous cut. Here the cut approaches the starting point.

Illus. 225. The completed sawing.

Illus. 226. The pattern can be easily removed even though it has remained tightly bonded throughout the sawing operation.

Illus. 227. A careful look at this project reveals inside openings that have more fragile projections than other inside openings. Cut the small openings of the body and frame first. The large central openings that include the left legs, lower flame, and lower head should be cut last.

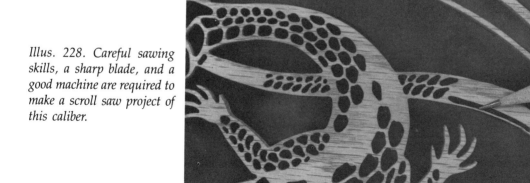

Illus. 228. Careful sawing skills, a sharp blade, and a good machine are required to make a scroll saw project of this caliber.

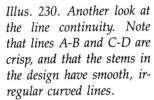

Illus. 229. Shown above are exaggerated imperfections that result from either a poor pattern or sloppy sawing. The lines below are accurate and crisp; note the line continuity of A to B.

Illus. 230. Another look at the line continuity. Note that lines A-B and C-D are crisp, and that the stems in the design have smooth, irregular curved lines.

Illus. 231. This project is a good example of how overall visual impact depends on successful employment of perfect line continuity in layout and sawing.

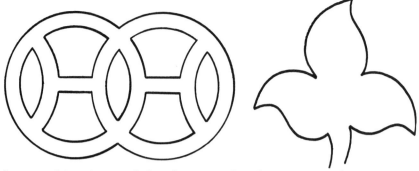

Illus. 232. A slight miscut on the geometrical design shown on the left will be far more noticeable than one on the leaf if it is not sawn perfectly.

your pattern, use a sharp, fine marking instrument. A fine, thin line is much easier to follow when sawing.

Check to see if the irregular curves that have to be sawn are drawn freeflowing and graceful. Does the pattern have to be corrected? Are the lines smooth and flowing when they change from one direction to another? If not, correct them freehand or use a French curve or a suitable template. An assortment of French curves and templates for circles, squares, and ellipses is very helpful.

It is difficult to hold the workpiece against a straight-edge sawing fence arrangement while sawing because the blade has a tendency to "float" or to follow the grain. Therefore, the fret worker usually relies on his hands and eyes for an accurate cut. Accurate cuts result from practice and experience, and confidence—when you know you can do something right, miscuts are rare.

Stack Cutting. Stack cutting, also known as

"plural cutting," is the process of sawing two or more pieces at once. (See Illus. 233.) It is done for two main reasons: To save time when applying patterns and drilling and sawing, and to increase the thickness of the material when very thin material is used.

The procedures for stack-sawing are as follow: Apply the pattern to just the top piece, place all parts to be cut one on top of the other, and fasten them securely together for sawing.

You can secure the stacked layers to each other in a variety of ways. One of the quickest and easiest ways is with nails. (See Illus. 234–236.) A conventional staple gun can be used in some instances. Illus. 237 shows it being used to staple thin plywood together. Use the proper thickness of plywood. If it is too thin, the staples will go completely through. If it is too thick, the staples won't reach.

Illus. 238–242 show stack-sawing techniques used to make two identical shelf

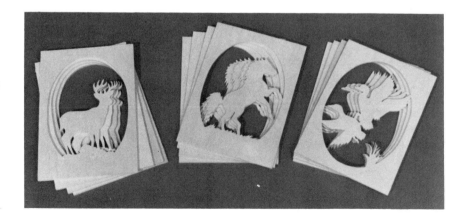

Illus. 233. Examples of stack cutting in which four identical pieces were produced for each pattern.

Illus. 234. These six layers of plywood have been secured together for stack sawing with small wire nails in the waste areas. Note that the inside cutouts are being sawn first.

Illus. 235. The resulting pieces. Note that different thicknesses and kinds of plywood were used.

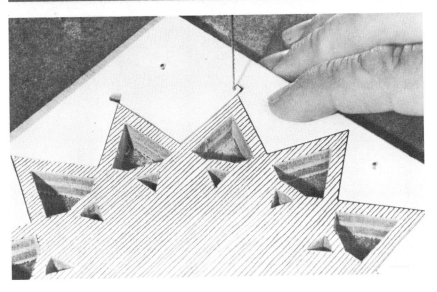

Illus. 236. Small brads hold these two layers of plywood together. Note that the inside openings were cut out first.

Illus. 237. These two pieces of thin material are being stapled together for stack cutting.

brackets from ¾-inch-thick material. Double-faced tape can be used to hold the layers of material together. (See Illus. 243 and 244.)

Another way of holding layers together is to apply glue, but only to the waste areas. One technique is to stack the pieces together, fasten them tightly, and then drill holes throughout all the pieces at once wherever you want a spot of glue. Spread a small amount on the surface around each hole of each layer, restack and press, and clamp or apply weight until the glue sets. Quick-setting adhesives or hot melts are the best glues to use.

If the pattern is fairly large, then also fasten the interior area of the stack layers. Also, make sure that each layer rests tightly on the layer underneath it; this is a means of avoiding vibration during sawing and minimizing any possible grain tear-out on bottom surfaces.

Do not overstack layers; this will prevent

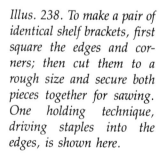

Illus. 238. To make a pair of identical shelf brackets, first square the edges and corners; then cut them to a rough size and secure both pieces together for sawing. One holding technique, driving staples into the edges, is shown here.

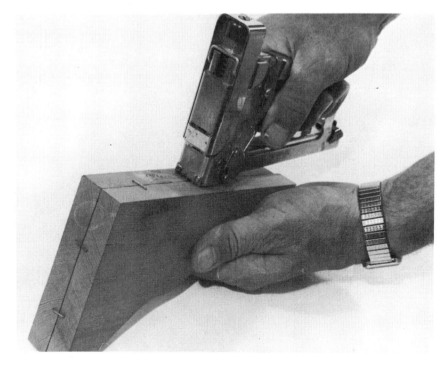

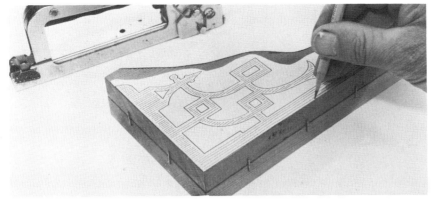

Illus. 239. The pattern is aligned with the two pre-sawn straight and squared edges, so those lines do not have to be cut with the scroll saw.

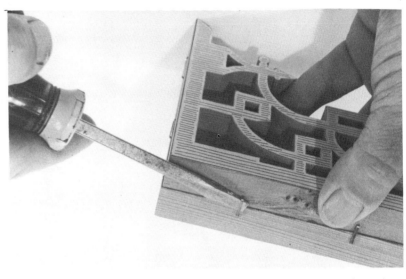

Illus. 240 (left). The bracket sawing time was cut in half by stack cutting. Illus. 241 (above). After sawing, you can easily remove the staples.

Illus. 242. The finished shelf with two identical brackets.

115

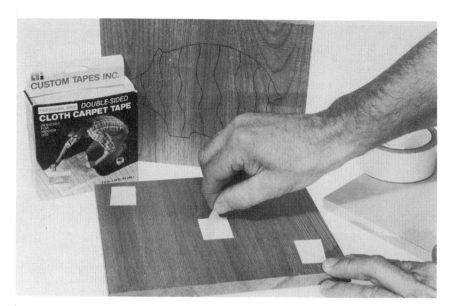

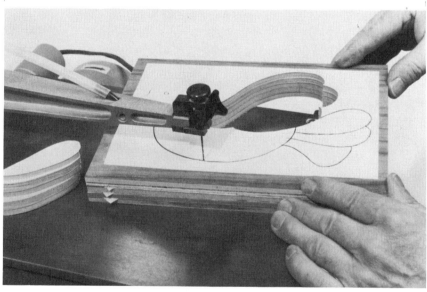

Illus. 243. Double-faced tape is being used here to hold layers of material together for stack sawing.

Illus. 244. You must often strategically locate small pieces of double-faced tape on each layer so that you can be sure that the stack doesn't come apart when certain parts of pattern are cut free. Here the pieces of tape are intentionally placed so that they are also visible at the lower left corner and at the opposite upper right corner.

you from sawing all layers uniformly. Stacking many layers of hardwood plywood, especially Baltic birch, may pose some problems. The many hard gluelines tend to dull blades very quickly.

Remember the following guidelines when stack-sawing: The blade must always be at a perfect 90-degree angle to the work. If not, the bottom layer will, obviously, not match the pattern. The thickness of the layers to be cut is limited by the thickness-cutting capac-

ity of the saw, how well the saw cuts hard or soft woods, and the number of pieces needed.

When stack-cutting, you can produce right- and left-hand pieces at the same time when needed. If you are using materials with only one good surface, place half of the good surfaces down (in the inner layers) and place half of the total number of pieces face-side up.

VI
SPECIAL TECHNIQUES

This chapter examines a variety of special techniques that the fret sawer should number among his repertoire of skills. Included here are overlaying and underlaying methods that incorporate various kinds of backgrounds, silhouettes and sign work, veining, carving picture and mirror framing, and architectural fretwork.

OVERLAYS

A standard overlay is essentially a thin decoration sawn from flat material and applied onto a solid background. A true fretwork overlay is not in any way three-dimensionally formed. However, carved frets can be used as overlays. Overlays can be used in a variety of situations to enhance fretwork. First, they can be used as ornaments for plain surfaces. They are an interesting departure from the cut-through designs of typical fretwork. Overlays can embellish doors, plain box lids, architectural and furniture panels, etc. (See Illus. 245 and 246.) In many instances, overlays are cut from woods that contrast with the background. This adds a special touch to fretwork. (See Illus. 247 and 248.) Overlays can also be used to conceal material imperfections and some structural elements such as certain joints. (See Illus. 249.)

During the past years, many different kinds of materials other than wood have been used as overlays, including brass, copper, ivory, and mother of pearl. There are many materials to choose from, so work with any material that interests you. In this chapter, however, only wood will be examined.

The size and the character of the design should determine the optimum thickness of the overlay material. Most fretworkers use wood that's too thick—resulting in a coarse, heavy look. As a general rule, the smaller and the more delicate the overlay, the thinner

Illus. 245. This shelf, made by Carl Weckhorst, features an overlay (bird) on a fretted background.

Illus. 246. Another shelf by Carl Weckhorst utilizes an overlay as a focal point.

Illus. 247 (above left). More overlay work by Carl Weckhorst. Illus. 248 (above right). A clock door overlay, also by Carl Weckhorst. Note how the design fits the door. The overlay material is 3mm plywood.

Illus. 249. Decorative overlays such as those on this frame can help to hide and strengthen joints.

it should be. Plywood ⅟₁₆ inch and 3 mm thick is usually a good choice. (See Chapter III, pages 77–80). Finnish birch and Baltic birch plywood make very suitable overlays. They are durable, yet have "soft" grain figures and colors that suggest an appropriate delicateness. The wild or coarse-grain figures on some woods prove to be unattractive when used in fretwork. Another general guideline to keep in mind is that overlays are usually made from a material that contrasts in color with the background of the fretted project. Light-colored overlays look good on almost all backgrounds. However, be careful when using dark overlays on light backgrounds—this could make the overlay appear heavy, which is contrary to the look you are trying to achieve. (See Illus. 250–252.)

Overlays should be cut carefully for three important reasons. One, the design of pattern is usually very delicate. Two, the material is thin and difficult to saw. Three, because the material will contrast with the background, mistakes will be obvious. (See Illus. 253 and 254.) When the overlay is delicate and the material is thin, a suitable fine blade will be necessary. You should sandwich thin material (⅟₁₆ or ³⁄₃₂ inch thick) between two waste boards while sawing. If you are cutting together several overlays in a stack, make sure that the top layer is strong and use a backer board to support the bottom.

Another factor to consider when using solid woods is the consistency of the grain direction, though your concern is limited only to how the pieces will look. (See Illus. 252 and 253). Since woods swell and shrink with changes in humidity, the grain of the overlay and the backer should run in the same direction.

Saw out the inside openings of larger intricate overlays first. Be careful when sawing up to narrow parts; you do not want the blade to inadvertently cut through. Saw carefully with a firm and easy feeding motion; press down the delicate areas near the blade with your fingers. If you experience problems with grain tear on the bottom surface, and fragile points are breaking off, try the following: Glue a tough but thin paper permanently onto the back of the overlay. You do not have to move the paper. Glue it to the background with the overlay.

Apply glue very carefully if the overlay is very delicate. Usually there are some larger areas where glue can be used a little more liberally, and small areas that should only be "spotted." One effective method for applying glue to the overlay is to first apply a thin coat of glue onto a piece of glass (or any smooth, flat material), drop the overlay on it, and then press gently to coat all areas. If careful when applying glue, you will save a lot of time cleaning up the excess glue that has oozed out around the edges. (See Illus. 255–260.)

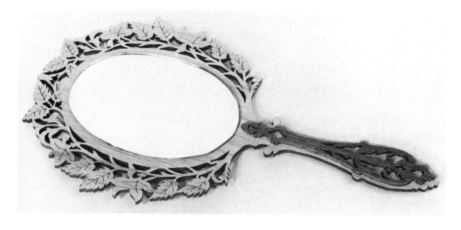

Illus. 250. This hand mirror by Carl Weckhorst incorporates two special techniques: the handle has an overlay, and the leaves have fine saw cuts (known as veining cuts).

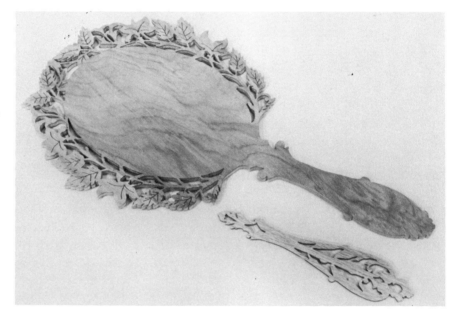

Illus. 251. The back side of the hand mirror will have a non-contrasting overlay (oak on birch).

Illus. 252. Note the letter S, which is an overlay of solid padauk on butternut. The grain of the overlay runs in the same direction as the background.

120

Illus. 253. Make the rough-ing-out cut with pattern on the wood, so that the grain runs in the right direction.

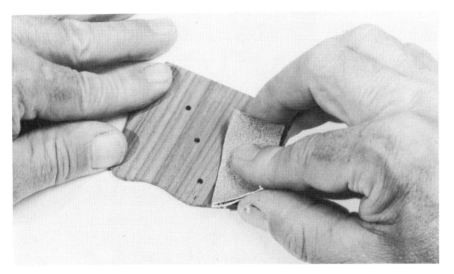

Illus. 254. After you have drilled the holes so that you can make the interior cut-outs, sand any grain tear on the back so that the work-piece will lay flat on the saw table during sawing.

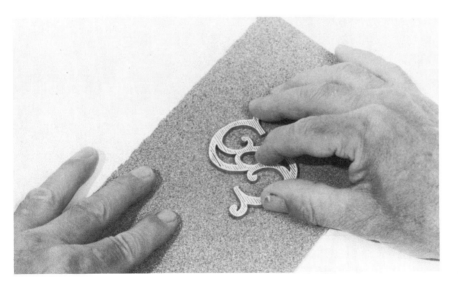

Illus. 255. Sand the cutout overlay (initial) by carefully moving it over sandpaper held stationary on a flat sur-face.

Illus. 256. Position the overlay on the backer and mark it with two distinct pencil points or pin pricks so that you can reposition it more easily. If you are going to stain the overlay, do it before gluing.

Illus. 257. One way to apply glue to the overlay is to spread an even coat of it onto a piece of plate glass or another smooth, flat surface.

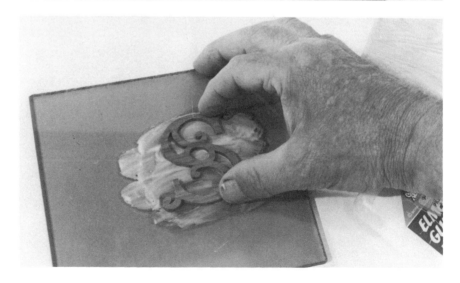

Illus. 258. Carefully lay the initial on the surface that has glue.

122

Illus. 259. Use a piece of plate glass or clear plastic to distribute pressure; this way, you can view the job.

Illus. 260. Remove any excess glue after it sets, but before it cures to a hardened form.

It can be difficult to position overlays, so make sure that you have pre-positioned your piece before applying glue. Before gluing, lay the overlay on the background and either mark with a pencil or pinprick two positioning points or set in three pins for guides when you lay the glue-applied overlay in place. After the overlay is glued in place, place something flat on it to distribute pressure and weigh it down. Use a heavy piece of plastic or waste plate glass (with smooth edges for safe handling). This way, you can see when the overlay moves or excess glue accumulates. Illus. 252–260 show the step-by-step procedures for making and gluing an overlay of an initial to a jewelry box.

Gold or silver escutcheon pins (decorative nails) can be used to fasten some overlays. Fine brass wood screws or fine brads can also be used; touch the brad heads with matching paint if they are noticeable. Pre-drill holes for all screw or nails. This is where a high-speed Dremel Moto-Tool or a similar tool is useful for drilling holes in fragile materials.

Underlaying for Overlays

There are several different ways to use overlays in fretwork. One way is to overlay with underlays. An underlay is a piece of wood fitted or inlaid into the background that contrasts with the applied overlay. In other words, an overlay is placed on top of a background that has one or more inlays set in it. The inlay will show through one or more of the overlay cutout openings. (See Illus. 261.)

Make sure that you select the right color combinations because at least three different colors are being dealt with. All the joints of the inlaid underlay have to be covered by the overlay.

Underlays are usually placed behind the larger openings of the fretted overlay. They do not have to be precisely fit at the edges as long as the overlay overlaps and conceals the edges. The inlay surfaces obviously must be set flush with the surface of the background.

When inlays are used, special techniques are applied to remove material from surfaces and make recessed openings for the fitted inlays. These procedures involve operations such as guided routing and/or careful hand chiselling partway into surfaces. Usually inlay work is similar to veneering and marquetry techniques. This is a technique that has to be treated thoroughly. For those seriously interested in inlaying solids or veneers, turn to books that deal entirely with these techniques.

Double Overlaying

Double overlaying is another technique that involves three layers of either three different types of wood or of any combinations of wood desired. (See Illus. 262 and 263.) Double overlays can be used more easily and quickly than underlaying techniques that depend upon the sizes and complexities of the elements involved. Double overlays can also enhance the look of the project by making it look deeper.

Background Plaques

Background plaques are sometimes required for certain fretted overlays, and are used on wall ornaments, silhouettes, signs, and clock faces. (See Illus. 264 and 265.) A background plaque protects fragile work. However, background plaques that are outlandish or wild-looking can detract from the fretwork's appearance. Background plaques

Illus. 261. An overlay with underlaying. The shaded areas are underlaid. An underlay is essentially an inlay set into the background before the overlay is applied.

Illus. 262. An example of a double overlay. Note the overlaid, ½ round purchased mould-ing that borders the overlaid panel.

Illus. 263. A closer look at the overlay work shown in Illus. 262. Note that the three woods used contrast with each other.

Illus. 264. Background plaques of various shapes can be used for fretwork overlays. Shape the edges with router or shaper if desired.

Illus. 265. A plain, contrasting background plaque sets off this lettering overlay designed by Kirk Ratajesak.

should be plain and not too finely detailed; in most cases, they should be shaped like the general outline of the fret. Illus. 264 shows a variety of traditional shapes. Any one can be enlarged to a size that satisfies your needs. A router-shaped edge, if made of solid woods, adds a nice touch to plaques; otherwise, simply cover plywood and fibreboard edges with an opaque finish.

Well-finished wood backgrounds are normally preferred, but you can use other materials such as velvet, silk, heavy paper, and leather on cheap backers to create some special effects.

SILHOUETTES

There are few articles made with the scroll saw that are more attractive or ornamental than silhouettes. (See Illus. 266–270.) The word silhouette can be traced back to an 18th century French minister of finance, Etienne Silhouette, who, because of national finance woes, encouraged thriftiness in the people. At the time, a certain type of art was popular in which profiles of a face were made by tracing a shadow cast on paper by a candle. The profiles were filled in with black. They were called Silhouettes.

Our companion book, *Scroll Saw Fretwork Patterns*, has a number of fretwork silhouettes. (Also see the patterns in Chapter IX.) To make a personal profile silhouette, use a strong light to cast a shadow onto paper. Trace the outline and reduce it to the size desired.

Baltic birch, Finland birch plywood, and any suitable sheet material can be used for silhouette work. Of course, the material should be sound and free of internal voids. Sheet material 1/32–1/4 inch thick can be used, including hardboard. If you want a black silhouette, you can paint the material before or after sawing.

Use fine blades and saw very carefully because imperfections will really stand out. Be sure to use stack-sawing techniques for production and multiple cuttings. Veining cuts can also be used on silhouettes and overlay work to accentuate certain features and details.

VEINING

Veining is simply the technique of sawing fine lines through the work to add more character to the design or to help emphasize certain parts. Illus. 267–269 and 271 show veined silhouettes. A fretsawn leaf, for example, looks much better when you saw hairline cuts on it that represent the veins of the leaf. (See Illus. 272.) The fenders and other parts on the car silhouette shown in Illus. 273

Illus. 266. Some basic silhouettes made by Kirk Ratajesak.

Illus. 267 (above left). This Joan of Arc silhouette by John Polhemus is accentuated with veining techniques. Note that some veining cuts originate in the interior, and some are cut inward from the outer edge. Illus. 268 (above right) A silhouette overlay enhanced with line work, veining, or woodburning.

Illus. 269. A small sil-houette with very fine vein-ing. Remember, veining is the sawing of a single line that is cut through the full thickness of the workpiece.

Illus. 270. Some miniature silhouette work sawn from thin plywood.

Illus. 271 (above left). The leaves on this wall shelf by Larry Boehner were accentuated with veining techniques. Illus. 272 (above right). A close up that shows the detail involved in extra-fine veining. Note the very small starting holes.

Illus. 273. (Photo courtesy of AMI Ltd.)

were designated with sawn lines. You can start the veining cuts entirely within the design itself or cut into the design by sawing inward from an outside edge. Interior veining is most effective when the blade entry hole is barely large enough to permit the blade to be threaded through the workpiece.

Normally, veining work is done with fine blades; the actual size blade used depends upon the thickness and character of the detail being cut. If the material is very thin, use a sharp knife to make very narrow, undetectable slits for each blade entry hole. A design, however, can appear confusing to the viewer if too many veining cuts are made.

LETTERING AND SIGN WORK

It is not difficult to produce lettering and sign work with a scroll saw. These two crafts provide a means of generating extra income. Sign work in some cases can become a lucrative business. Scores of commercially made lettering templates, sign layout guides, and alphabet patterns are available to help both beginners and professional scroll sawers. *Scroll Saw Fretwork Patterns* has some full-size alphabet patterns and sign board designs.

Though almost any wood can be used out-side as long as it is properly sealed, finished, and positioned so that it is protected from the elements, carefully select and plan how to use the wood. Outdoor signs have to withstand the ravages of the environment. Sun, rain, snow, ice, and wind can be devastating to wood signs if they are not made from the proper woods and assembled properly. As a general rule, cedar, cypress, and redwood are good woods to use if you live in a region that receives a lot of rain or snow. Exterior and or marine plywoods make good backings on which to attach cutout letters. Do not apply clear varnishes or lacquers to outside signs because the sun can rapidly degrade clear, nonpenetrating finishes.

Interior signs can be made of any wood as long as it looks good, is seasoned for indoor use, and can be cut with a scroll saw. (Refer to *Making Wood Signs* and *Alphabets and Designs for Wood Signs*, both by Sterling Publishing Co., for basic information on all aspects of sign work.)

Scroll saw signs can be made in several ways. The letters can be pierced or cut out of the background, as shown in Illus. 274–276. They can also be made with no or open backgrounds, as shown in Illus. 277 and 278. In another method, individually sawn letters

Illus. 274. This interior sign, made of mahogany by John Polhemus, is a good example of pierced letter work.

Illus. 275. A close-up look at pierced art detail and lettering.

Illus. 276. A clock face by Carl Weckhorst that features pierced numbers and overlay ornamentation.

Illus. 277. This sign by Kirk Ratajesak, does not have any background; the individual letters are joined together with a minimum of ties.

Illus. 278. Lettering with the entire background removed.

can be overlaid on a background, as shown in Illus. 279 and 280.

Combining Fretwork and Carving

Some fretworkers practice a combination of fretwork and carving. They believe that carving the outlines on fretwork accentuates them and makes the piece more attractive. Typical carving techniques include carving leaves with gouges, making the veins in leaves with parting or veining tools, and giving rounded or half-round forms to stems, fruits, and berries, as shown in Illus. 282.

Fretwork is basically flat ornamentation with the design expressed in the profile or silhouette. Carving shows the design in relief. Some fretworkers feel that they are two different crafts, and should not be incorporated into one technique. They would rather accentuate the delicate features on fretwork

Illus. 279. The individual letters on this sign were overlaid or mounted to a solid backing.

Illus. 280. An incredibly ambitious scroll-sawn sign by Carl Weckhorst. All the art lettering is overlaid onto a solid panel backing.

Illus. 281 (below left). Another clock face by Carl Weckhorst. This one features individual overlaid numbers on a contrasting wood. Illus. 282. (below right). An ordinary wall shelf bracket of currents and leaves. The front piece, which supports the shelf, is exactly one-half the thickness of the back piece. Both pieces can be sawed at once, with the bracket on top of the pattern. The veins of the leaves can be carved in, and the stems and berries rounded.

WALL BRACKET.

TABLE EASEL.

Illus. 283. The ribbons on this project, which was fret sawed and carved, appear to pass over and under each other.

Illus. 284 (right). A finely detailed fretwork clock by Carl Weckhorst with a simple carved bird overlay (above). Note the use of beaded mouldings.

Illus. 285. A close-up of the clock shown in Illus. 284 reveals the carved bird, mouldings, and how the upper section is made separately to sit on top.

Illus. 286 (far left). Another Weckhorst project combining many techniques, including some overlay carving. Illus. 287 (left). A close-up of the carved deer head overlay. Note the simply sawn leaf veining.

with a scroll saw instead of through carving.

In some instances, carved overlays can emphasize one part of a project or add an intriguing dimension to the entire project without detracting from the surrounding fretwork. Illus. 284–286 show some of Carl Weckhorst's fretwork pieces, which have simple rounded carvings. Mr. Weckhorst rounded over the edges of overlays sawn from solid woods, added some details to them and then glued them to the felt backing.

Commercially carved or embossed ornaments and mouldings of many designs and configurations can be purchased and applied to projects, if so desired. Illus. 288 shows just a few of the many designs available.

MAKING FRAMES

It takes a few specialized, but easy, techniques to make frames for photographs, mirrors, wall hangings, and silhouettes with just the scroll saw. Because most fret-sawn objects are made from thin materials, one or more simple overlays are used to form the recess or rabbeted lip openings that hold the photograph, glass, or mirror and the backing. (See Illus. 289.) If you are using thicker wood for the frames, then use a router (if available) with a rabbeting bit to create the inside lip necessary to support the material being framed.

Gluing an ornamental or plain oval (round) rim or straight strip overlay to the front surface reduces the size of the sawn opening, thus creating the inside rabbet or lip. Illus. 290–292 depict this technique, with simple, flat moulding being used as the overlay. Use a typical backer-supporting material such as cardboard or hardboard to hold the photo and the glass in place. Hold the cardboard and/or hardboard itself in place with small brads, points, clips, or masking tape.

Illus. 288. Some examples of commercially carved or embossed mouldings.

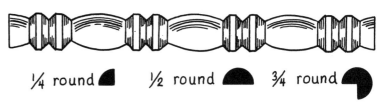

¼ round   ½ round   ¾ round

½ round

Illus. 289. Photo frames with overlays that are used to create rabbeted (recessed) openings.

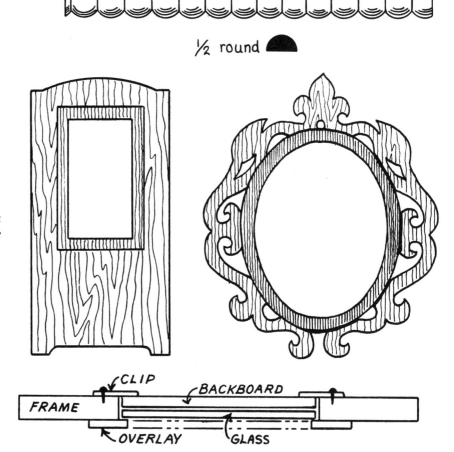

CLIP

BACKBOARD

FRAME

OVERLAY

GLASS

Illus. 290. The simple flat mouldings overlaid onto the front surface of these frames proved to be both decorative and functional.

Illus. 291. A close-up of the flat strip overlay that overlaps the opening to the table.

Illus. 292. The back view of the fret-sawn frame and the rabbeted lip created by the overlapping of the strip moulding overlay.

Illus. 293 and 294 show another framing method, called "back-framing." The overlay or "stick" frame is attached to the back surface of the fretted project. The back overlaid frame does not overlap the opening, but instead is set away from it as shown in Illus. 293, to create a rabbeted lip. This technique can be carried a step further if you eliminate the top piece of the rear frame so that you can slip a backer (with a thumb slot) in from the top. (See Illus. 294.)

Objects can be frame-mounted to a surface with double-frame overlays. (See Illus. 295.) If you use this technique, you do not have to saw an opening. Leave the outer edges of the frames straight or saw them to add a decorative touch. The double-frame overlay technique is good for face-frame-mounting bevelled edge mirrors and other typically flat objects. If you use decorative screws, you can make the outer frame so that it is removable.

You will have to use a rear supporting leg or strut to make photo frames that will remain freestanding on a mantel or table top. (See Illus. 296.) The supporting strut must be secure (must not slip) and must tilt the frame back to the ideal viewing angle. A bevelled block (Illus. 296) meets these requirements, but you can also use a decorative retaining chain to connect the strut leg and the back of the frame.

PIERCING WORK

Piercing work adds a fresh, interesting look to many projects. Piercing frets, like those shown in Illus. 297, can be used in numerous ways to effectively embellish plain monotonous furniture and cabinet panels.

In true fretwork piercing, you cut the design itself away from the solid background. This differs from typical fretwork, in which you cut the background away from the design. Illus. 297 shows a sign with pierced letters.

CHIPPENDALE FRETS

Chippendale frets and continuous trim, are used to add a special look to furniture rails, grills, overlays, and some interior architectural applications. (See Illus. 298.) These frets are typically geometrically induced designs that are repeated, usually in a linear direction. Some are designed to be endless.

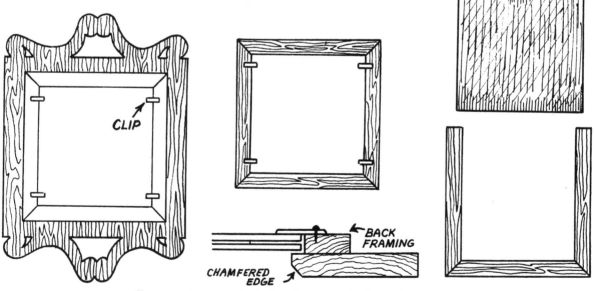

Illus. 293 (above left). Typical "back framing" details. Illus. 294 (above far right). Eliminating the top piece of back framing allows you to insert the photo, glass, backer, etc., from the top.

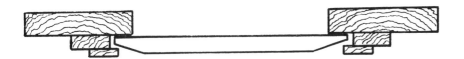

Illus. 295. Double overlay face framing.

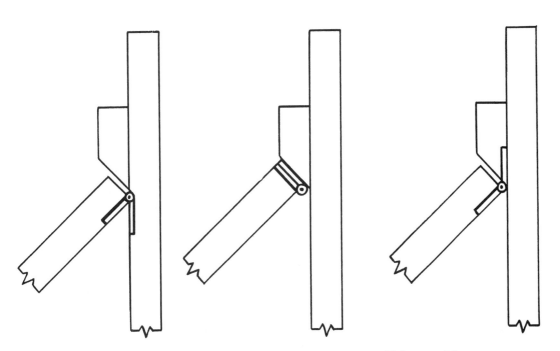

Illus. 296. Three methods of mounting photo frame strut (leg) hinges. If the materials are too thin for screws, use leather or another hinging material. Glue the leather- or fabric-type hinges, as shown at the right; lay the material under all of the beveled block.

Illus. 297. Some design examples of furniture piercings.

Illus. 298. Sawing Chippendale frets and long-running fretted trim presents some problems.

It may be difficult to saw these long and narrow workpieces because the throat on most scroll saws is limited for this class of work. If you are using narrow blades, you can often cut the work from another direction when the workpiece hits the rear of the machine by making an "on-the-spot" turn and attempting the cut from the opposite side of the saw arm. An alternative technique is reinstalling the blade so that it's rearwards—that is, its teeth face the rear of the machine. This technique, however, is awkward, but with a little practice you will be able to do it successfully, especially if you use spiral blades. Spiral blades cut in all directions, though they are more difficult to handle on straight line work because they follow the grain of the wood rather than the pattern line.

Sometimes, however, the fretwork is designed in such a way that you can cut out shorter segments and butt them end to end. This technique works if you use such frets for overlays or otherwise attach them to some back support.

It is possible on most machines to saw pieces that are longer than the machine's throat capacity. The Sears and Dremel saws have four-position blade holders, which help to facilitate these types of cuts. You can use other saws to cut in a band-saw fashion (sideways feeding) by simply twisting the top and bottom end of your saw blades with a pair of pliers. Refer to your owner's manual or the *Scroll Saw Handbook* for more information. Another viable approach—especially when sawing Chippendale-style and long-running frets—is to stack-cut a number of pieces at one time, and then place the parts end to end to make longer frets.

ARCHITECTURAL FRETWORK

Architectural fretwork includes a wide variety of designs that are used for home or commercial interiors (Illus. 299–302) and exteriors. The highly ornamental Victorian-style of fretwork became popular in the early 1800s, and continued in popularity for almost 100 years. This form of elaborate decorative woodworkings has once again undergone a resurgence in popularity. It is being used in restored or remodelled structures and also incorporated into present-day architecture.

Architectural fretwork, also called Victorian Gingerbread or Carpenter's Lace, is cut from various kinds of woods that range in thickness anywhere from ½ inch for interior

Illus. 299 (left). An interior corner bracket. Illus. 300 (above). A fretted arch can be used in several locations, such as over the kitchen sink.

Illus. 301 (above left). A fretted "interior medallion" panel combines turnings and sawn fretwork. (Photo courtesy of Cumberland Woodcraft Co., Inc., Carlisle, Pennsylvania) Illus. 302 (above right). This interior grill is an interesting combination of spindle work and fretwork. (Photo courtesy of Cumberland Woodcraft Co., Inc., Carlisle, Pennsylvania)

scrolls to as much as 4 inches for some exterior scrolls. (See Illus. 303–306.) Obviously, the work you can do is limited by the thickness-cutting capacity of your saw. However, you can always cut parts individually, and glue-laminate the sawn parts together to increase the thickness. You can level or correct minor irregularities between layers with good wood fillers and conceal them with a top coat of paint.

Much of the finer sawn work was often combined with turnings. That's why many of the old scroll saws with small lathe attachments (illustrated in Chapter 1) were popular.

Architectural fretwork is even being used in model buildings and dollhouses (See Illus. 307–310.)

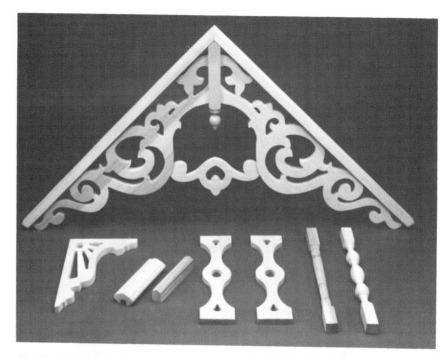

Illus. 303. This fretted gable bracket and other exterior trim were made by Cumberland Woodcraft Co., Inc., Carlisle, Pennsylvania.

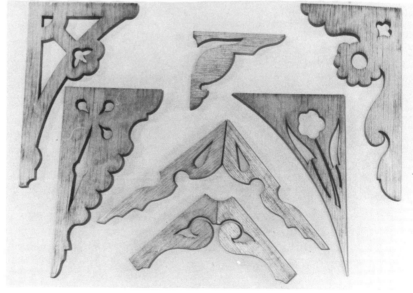

Illus. 304. Some typical exterior brackets cut from thick pine.

Illus. 305 (above left). A typical porch post bracket. Illus. 306 (above right). Fretwork can be used to decorate screen or storm doors. (Photo courtesy of Cumberland Woodcraft Co., Inc., Carlisle, Pennsylvania)

Illus. 307. These miniature fretwork brackets used for doll house trim were made by Kirk Ratajesak.

*Illus. 308. A model of a cha-
let with fretted architectural
trim.*

*Illus. 309. A closer look at
the model chalet, which was
made of cedar. Note the roof
trim, porch baluster, and
window valances.*

*Illus. 310. Stairway rail bal-
usters and a "lazy" way to
make steps for the chalet
model.*

144

VII
JOINTS AND ASSEMBLY TECHNIQUES

Strong, well-executed joints are as essential in fretwork as they are in fine furniture-making, cabinetry, and other woodcrafts. Regardless of how expertly and carefully the profile fret sawing is done, it cannot overshadow or conceal careless assembly work.

Thinly cut fretwork pieces are delicate and are not required to withstand heavy loads or excessive strain. Consequently, the simplest types of joints are usually satisfactory and should be used wherever possible. Today's modern adhesives and mechanical fasteners provide a simple means of joining and strengthening the joint. This was not true in years past. Joints that interlocked, such as dovetails and mortise-and-tenon joints, were necessary because effective wood-to-wood joining supplies were not available.

In this chapter, a wide variety of joints and joining practices will be illustrated. It also includes some "old-fashioned" techniques for those who want to make authentic reproductions from older patterns and designs. Some of the joints recommended for certain projects can be made entirely with the scroll saw itself.

TYPES OF JOINTS

Tab and Slot Joint

Tab-and-slot joints are a form of mortise-and-tenon joint. In fact, some fretworkers use these terms interchangeably. When varieties of these joint are assembled, they are hidden (not visible). Other types, often called "through" or "open" mortise-and-tenon joints, are not hidden. Illus. 311–318 show various applications and projects on which basic mortise-and-tenon or tab-and-slot joints are used.

Some cabinetmakers and expert craftsmen are familiar with the more complex shouldered (haunched) and wedged variations of the mortise-and-tenon joint, but these joints, as a rule, are seldom used by fretsawers. In fact, very often simple butt joints strengthened with nails or screws and glue are used instead of mortise-and-tenon joints.

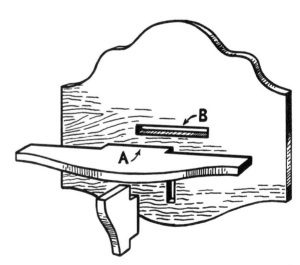

Illus. 311. The simplest form of the mortise (B) and tenon (A) joint, as shown here, is typical of the joint found in many foreign patterns. When properly made, this joint is not easily detected.

145

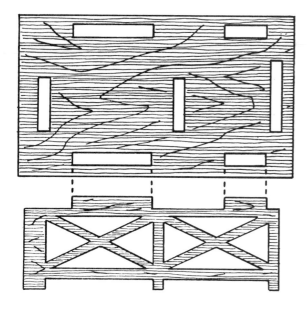

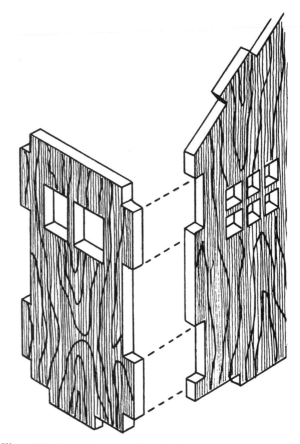

Illus. 312. Some patterns specify mortise-and-tenon joints for virtually every piece of the entire project. This requires a very careful layout and accurate straight-line cutting. You can often modify such patterns to incorporate simpler butt joints that are faster and easier to make and assemble.

Illus. 313. Certain open tab-and-slot joints, such as the ones designed for this outside corner of a model building, are not intended to be hidden. Some tab-and-slot joints are also used to disassemble and reassemble certain projects such as toys and dollhouses.

Illus. 314. A simple slotted joint used in a napkin/letter holder project.

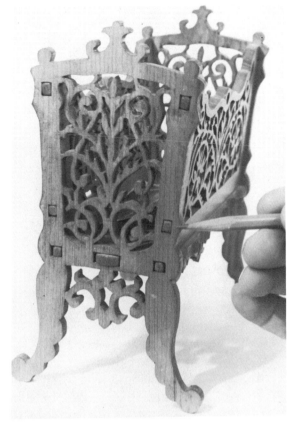

Illus. 315. This toy cradle made by Carl Weckhorst is designed with visible through mortise-and-tenon joints.

Illus. 316. A closer look shows how the two sides and the bottom are tenoned into square, open mortises on the two end pieces.

Illus. 317. This lidded basket is made entirely of open mortise-and-tenon construction.

Illus. 318. The lids hinge on dowel pivots. Note that the through tenons can extend further than just the thickness of the mortised pieces, and that their ends can also be decorative.

Halved Joints

Halved joints (Illus. 319–321) can also be machined entirely with the scroll saw, but must be laid out and sawn very carefully. Make sure that you have sawn the parts just slightly oversize so that they can slide into each other without being forced—especially when you are using solid wood. In some cases, the slightest pressure may split the wood. On the other hand, take into account the fact that if you are going to sand the faces, you will reduce the thicknesses and the needed widths of the openings. In fact, sometimes, depending upon the character of the design, it may be more advantageous to saw the halved slots before sawing any of the remaining fret profiles. Often, a long halved slot temporarily weakens the fret, in which case the slot should not be cut until last. Remember that the quickest and easiest way to attain a perfect fit with all such joints is to carefully lay out the joints and then saw them very accurately.

Locked Tab-and-Slot Joint

The locked tab-and-slot joint is another joint where the mating parts can also be sawn entirely with the scroll saw. This joint is somewhat of a compromise between the plain tab-and-slot joint and the halved joint. (See Illus. 322–325.) It is somewhat difficult to lay out because the slots have to be set

slightly off the tabs, as can be seen in Illus. 325. Locked tab-and-slot joints are good to use in various utility-type projects and in toymaking when building and dismantling play barns, fences, models, bridges, boxes, etc. It also should be mentioned that plywood is an especially good material to use when you are incorporating this joint into projects that will be roughly used, like toys.

Miscellaneous Joints

Since the fretworker is often involved with cabinetry and fine-furniture work, some knowledge of various framing joints and the common kinds of right-angle joints is helpful. (See Illus. 326 and 327.) When you are making these joints, it is always helpful if you have access to other shop machinery such as the table saw and jointer, and the router is always welcomed. Be certain that you know the safety procedures involved in using such tools. Also be well aware that serious accidents are more likely to occur when you are machining small and thin materials.

The butt joint is usually glued and nailed. This joint is usually not preferred when plywood is being used. Various rabbeted joints are good to use because much less end grain or plywood edge is visible. Two good variations of the rabbeted joint are those made with a round over or a bead. In both cases, the amount of end grain that is visible is minimized.

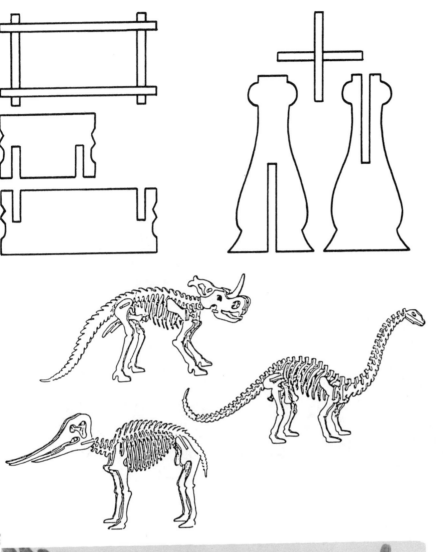

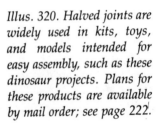

Illus. 319. Halved joints. The joints on the left are used for the sides of a box. Those on the right are used to make the central joint of a stand or base.

Illus. 320. Halved joints are widely used in kits, toys, and models intended for easy assembly, such as these dinosaur projects. Plans for these products are available by mail order; see page 222.

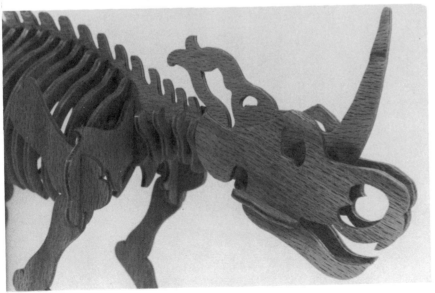

Illus. 321. This close-up shows how the halved joints on each piece or part give this project a three-dimensional quality.

Illus. 322 (above left). This entire project can be assembled or disassembled with locked tab-and-slot joints. Illus. 323 (above right). Here you can see how the back, with integral corner brackets (above), interlocks with the sides to keep the project from "racking" from side to side.

Illus. 324. Here are all the parts for the project shown in Illus. 322 and 323. Note the tabs (with short locking slots) on the back and on the three shelf pieces. The two sides have conventional slots, but are positioned so that when the shelf tabs are inserted through and then moved sideways (to lock), the shelf will be properly positioned in relation to the back piece of the project.

Illus. 325. A closer look at two shelf tabs extending through the sides and then pulled forward to lock. Note the resulting openings behind each tab. This is one disadvantage of this type of joint, which is otherwise useful and very strong.

Illus. 326. Some basic right angle joints include the following: on top line, from left to right, butt, splined butt, dado-rabbet, and rabbet joint; on bottom line, from left to right, dado, mitre, rabbeted with roundover, and rabbeted with bead.

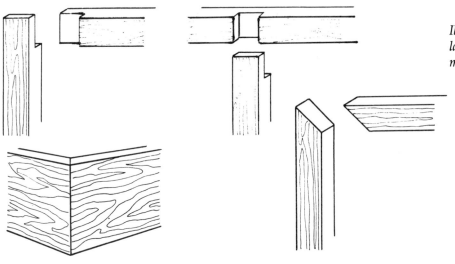

Illus. 327. Shown at top are lap joints. Shown below are mitre joints.

Illus. 328. A good example of a perfect, glued mitre joint. Note how clean and tight this joint in ¼-inch solid walnut is. A less-than-perfect joint in this situation would be totally unacceptable.

Mitre joints are used when you do not want to expose end grain or plywood edge at all. (See Illus. 328.) Mitre joints are generally weaker than other joints such as the nailed butt joint. However, if the bevelled surfaces of the mitre joint are cleanly cut and fit tightly to each other, then the glued joint will have sufficient strength.

SHOOTING BOARD

The shooting board is a homemade accessory that has many uses for all woodworkers. (See Illus. 329–335.) It is especially practical for the fretworker who must frequently cut and fit small pieces very accurately. The shooting board supports the workpieces while you use your hand plane to produce square and a variety of bevelled edges. The plane lays on its side and cuts the edge of the workpiece as it extends over the edge of the adjustable support piece. (See Illus. 331.)

The shooting board can be used to cut chamfers and to make flat or compound mitres that fit perfectly. Hold the workpiece and any supporting or angular blocks together with one hand as you work the hand plane with the other. Secure the blocks with double-faced tape if you are going to extensively use one setup.

The shooting board is obviously much

Illus. 329. The shooting board with a small "block plane." Use a larger plane for longer and thicker pieces. Here the support board is in a flat or horizontal position.

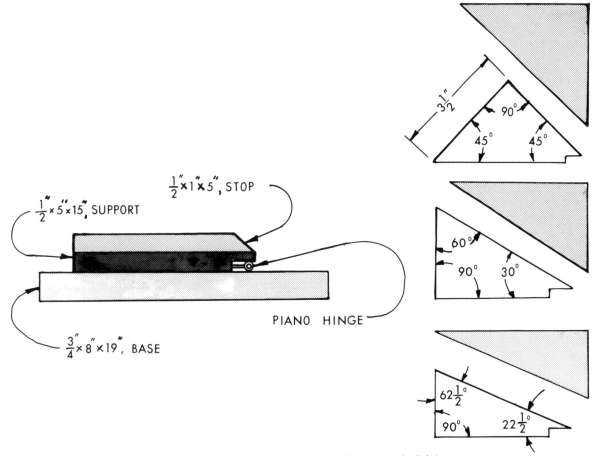

Illus. 330. The basic details for making the hinged shooting board. Shown on the left is an end view of the essential parts; shown on the right are some of the angle blocks that can be used with it.

Illus. 331. Here the shooting board is being used to make a flat mitre with a block plane. Notice the angle block inserted between the stop and the edge of the work-piece.

Illus. 332. The shooting board can be set to any inclined position if the appropriate support block is used.

Illus. 333. A look at the rear side of the shooting board and an interchangeable support block. Note that the full thickness of the hinge is rabbeted into upper piece.

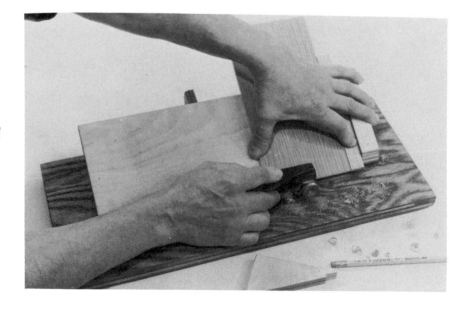

Illus. 334. Planing an end bevel square to an edge.

safer than a table saw or jointer, and it produces equally precise results. In fact, the shooting board should be used to prepare and true very small pieces that would be extremely dangerous and perhaps impossible to handle if machined on a jointer or table saw.

Make the shooting board carefully with a good table saw. If you don't have a table saw, hire someone to cut the parts for you. Hardwood veneer plywood is recommended, preferably Baltic birch because it is hard and stays flat.

Illus. 330 gives all the essential details for making a shooting board. It does not have to

be hinged, but if it isn't, it can only be used for squaring and to make simple flat mitres. You can make shooting boards of any size or length, but make sure that the base has a suitable allowance so that it can be clamped to a table or workbench.

STICK MOULDINGS

If you do own a table saw, you can make slotted corner mouldings with which to assemble fretted panels. Illus. 336 and 337 show how Carl Weckhorst fastened together four tapered panels with simple self-made mouldings to make an unusual lampshade.

Illus. 336. A lampshade project in progress by Carl Weckhorst.

155

Illus. 337. A top view of Weckhorst's lampshade project shows that slotted stick mouldings are being used for assembly.

FASTENING METHODS

Nails, screws, and glue are typical fastening methods that do not require special tools, but should be used with a certain amount of proficiency. Wire nails, brads, and brass nails are available in any size from ¼ inch in length and upward. Drive in small nails of this kind with a hammer that is smaller than the usual carpenter's or household hammer. (See Illus. 342.) Always drill small pilot holes for nails, especially when nailing into the edges of thin stock and/or all hardwoods. (See Illus. 341.) Do not hold very small nails with your fingers; this is often very awkward and hazardous. Use a thin strip of paper to help get the nail into an upright position. Push the nail through the end of the strip of paper. Place the nail in position, tap it until it stands by itself, and then tear away the paper. You can also use a thin magnet instead of a nail if you have one.

A screw is used differently than a nail. A nail is driven into both pieces of wood to hold them to each other. A screw, on the other hand, fits freely through a hole in the first piece of wood; then, by means of the screw thread, it draws or pulls the second piece of wood against the first. Most woodworking books discuss screw sizes and provide pilot and anchor hole sizes for various screws. If you do not have access to these books, measure the shank diameter of the screw (located under the head) and drill a test hole to be sure that the shank fits through easily. Flathead screws should be countersunk with a special bit. Roundhead screws are not usually recessed or set below the surface. (See Illus. 338.)

The glues and gluing techniques used vary with the type of project and the experience of the builder. There are many glues available that range from the typical liquid white polyvinyls to the yellow carpenter's glues to the "super" or other specialized glues. (See Illus. 339.) Glue joints are at their strongest when the pieces are made to fit tightly. You have to use a special "technique" to glue end grains and plywood edges. When gluing mitres and some other joints, coat both surfaces of the joint; double coat them if the glue penetrates the end grains too quickly.

Most beginners have problems dealing with the excess glue that is squeezed out of the joints. When they wipe it up, they drive glue into the surface of the wood along the joint. Such glue-coated areas will not take stains or finishes like raw wood does. This is a potentially devastating situation. *Gluing and Clamping*, Sterling Publishing Co., provides a lot of helpful information that will aid you in this situation and many others.

PROJECT ASSEMBLY

A typical small-fretwork wall-clock project is assembled in several different steps. Illus. 340–351 demonstrate how to nail this project together. You can use some of the techniques shown in this sequence to assemble other projects. Obviously, quick-setting glues could be substituted entirely or used with nails.

MISCELLANEOUS HARDWARE

You often have to use miscellaneous hard-

ware to add a final touch to a project. (See Illus. 352–355.) This may include various hinges, hooks, hasps, hangers, clips, pulls, and locks. Also available are specialty items such as brass ornaments, lamp parts, musical movements, weather instruments, thermometer cards, and clocks that will give your projects a professional look. Many well-stocked hardware and crafts shops carry most of the items you might need.

Illus. 338. The small round-head brass screws used to assemble this hard, thin cherry wood have to be drilled carefully so that the wood does not split.

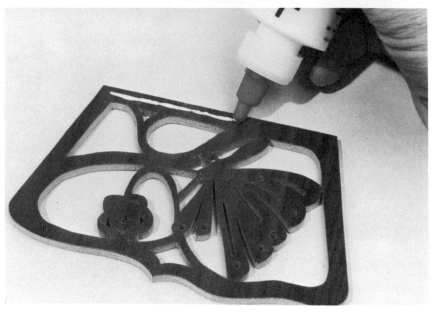

Illus. 339. The use of quick-drying glues can speed and simplify many fretwork assemblies and provide more than sufficient strength.

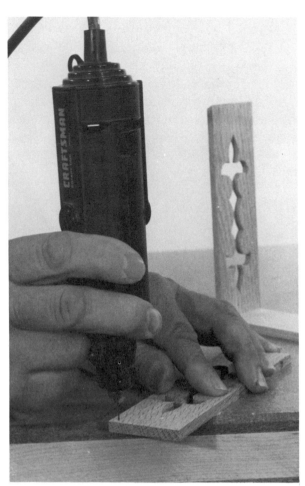

Illus. 340 (above left). Various methods and materials can be used to assemble this clock project of oak. Complete full-size patterns for this project are shown on pages 181–184. Illus. 341 (above right). Here a high-speed rotary tool is being used to drill the hard oak sides to eliminate possible splitting.

Illus. 342. Nailing the sides to a bottom. Note the small hammer being used.

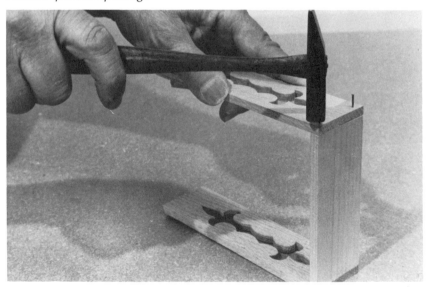

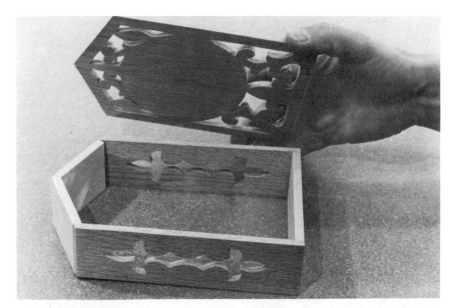

Illus. 343. Checking the fit of the front to the box frame parts.

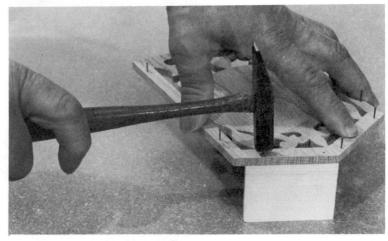

Illus. 344 (left). Locate and make starting points for the drill with a scratch awl. Illus. 345 (above). Nailing the face (front piece) to the upper frame pieces.

Illus. 346. The front and box frame assembled with brads and glue.

Illus. 347. Always drill. The short grain of the hardwood shown here is certain to split during nailing if it is not drilled.

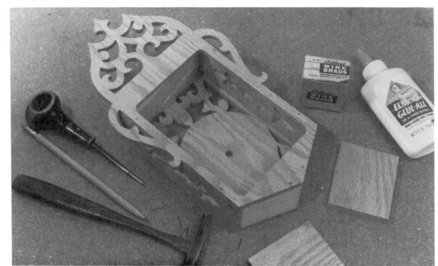

Illus. 348. Glue and nail on the back. Do not apply too much glue.

Illus. 349. The top (gable) decorative piece is attached next.

Illus. 350. Set all the nail holes, apply the finish, and insert the battery-powered clock.

Illus. 351. The time ring has its own pressure-sensitive adhesive backing.

Illus. 352. Special hardware can be obtained locally or by mail order. The glass thermometer shown here is mounted on a gold foil-faced card, which is simply glued to the wood.

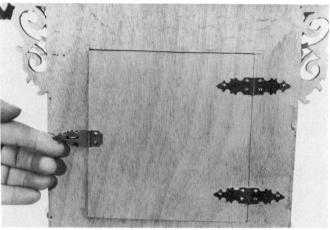

Illus. 353 (left). Special small hinges and catches suitable for mounting on thin materials are readily available from most conventional sources. Illus. 354 (above). Inexpensive decorative hinges and a hasp are used on the back door of this clock cabinet.

Illus. 355. With a paper template, you can accurately place these individual numbers with self-adhesive backing.

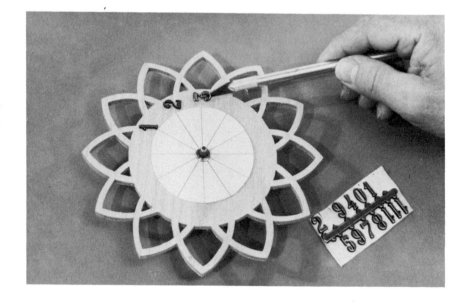

VIII
FINISHING FRETWORK

Fretwork projects are finished in generally the same way as other types of fine wood-craft. In fact, you may already have a finishing "system" that will work equally well on fretted projects. However, one primary difference is that fretted work consists of numerous openings and broken surfaces, which means that there are small areas and wood edges to contend with.

There are many good books devoted entirely to the subject of wood finishing, so .there is no need to dwell so comprehensively on it in this chapter. However, there are some guidelines and procedures that you should be aware of. Remember the following general rules: One of the keys to good wood finishing is the material you select for the project. (See Illus. 356.) Good-quality woods simply finish better and easier. They also are more attractive than cheaper species or lower-grade saw millings. Also, sand and prepare the surface well after selecting the wood but before sawing. Remove all mill marks, scratches, and other blemishes. If you apply the patterns correctly with the proper spray adhesives, they should not hinder your sanding and subsequent finishing efforts.

Following is an overview of finishing procedures and an examination of the best finishes to use for the material selected.

PREPARING THE WOOD

Preparing the wood for a finish involves any final touch-up necessary to smooth out

Illus. 356. Though walnut fretwork looks great with almost all finishes, a high-gloss-type finish would detract from this naturally rich, elegant look.

profile cuts, as well as the final sanding, in which you smooth the surface and remove the remaining pencil marks or glue spotting.

If you have used a good wood, and have sawed carefully with the correct blades, there should not be much to repair. However, you may have occasionally made a misguided, stray cut, chipped off material, broken off a small projection, or drilled in the wrong place.

If you are piecing-in matching scrap wood to fill a hole or to repair a wayward cut, be very careful when gluing it. Any excess glue remaining on visible surfaces will seal the wood so that finishes do not penetrate. This will result in some ugly-looking areas that will be difficult to fix. The same principle applies when using wood fillers. If you must use a filler to cover nails, holes, or another blemish, pick one that matches the wood finish and apply it after or just before the final finish coat. Do not apply it when the wood is still in its raw state; the filler will not take a stain or finish well even though many man-ufacturers claim that their fillers can be stained or finished.

Small files can sometimes be used to quickly improve the line continuity of profile cuts. (See Illus. 357.) However, don't make filing a common practice. It is a practice that should be kept separate from fretwork.

If a line can be corrected with a file, it can also be corrected with a scroll saw. Rethread the blade and carefully trim the imperfection. Sometimes careful use of a sharp jack knife, razor blade, X-acto knife, or even sandpaper glued to thin pieces of wood may be more helpful than a file.

SANDING

Fretwork is fragile and must be sanded carefully. If you have a good saw and have used the proper blade, you should not have much sanding to do along the sawn surfaces.

Illus. 357. Though a line can sometimes be improved if it is filed, files should not as a rule be used for smoothing sawn surfaces or for removing frayed fibres at the edges.

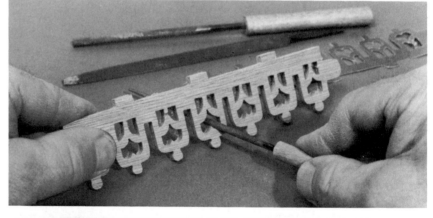

Illus. 358. Do all surface sanding before making any cuts. The final touch-up sanding after sawing should be done carefully, with the work supported on a flat surface. Sawn edges normally do not need sanding. The only real sanding should be to remove fibres that may remain along the cut and, more frequently, on the bottom surfaces.

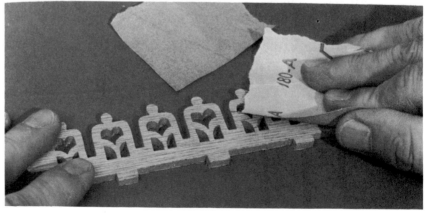

164

A residue of wood fibre normally remains along the edge. You can remove it easily by lightly sanding the surface with 180- to 220-grit surfaces.

A new piece of sandpaper is stiffer, stronger, and cuts faster, but worn pieces are often better because they are more flexible and dip more easily in the smaller cutouts. Apply the sandpaper with your fingers instead of using sanding blocks. (See Illus. 358.) Sanding blocks aren't useful at all.

When using sandpaper, separate those used on dark and light woods. Fine dust from dark woods such as walnut and rosewood can color lighter woods during sanding.

STAINING AND FINISHING

Stain solid woods and plywoods carefully, and only after you have made appropriate tests on some identical scrap. Plywood and solid end-grain edges will absorb too much of a stain if special, precautionary steps are not taken. The surfaces of many softwoods such as pine, inexpensive grades of Baltic birch, and cheaper plywood often absorb stains erratically, which results in an undesirable blotchy look. (See Illus. 359.)

Glossy or highly polished finishes are not appropriate for most fretwork. They are difficult to apply smoothly or uniformly by hand and are normally best left for use on flat, unbroken surfaces. Penetrating finishes are, as a rule, the easiest to apply—more so than conventional surface finishes like varnish, polyurethane, and lacquer.

Only use paints and enamels on exterior architectural fretwork, toys, models, and similar projects. When finishing exterior fretwork, soak it in a penetrating wood preservative such as Woodlife or Thompson's Wood Seal prior to painting. This can improve the service life of the project. Almost all other

Illus. 359. Shown here are stained and natural finishes on the same birch. Note the "smudged" look in the stained example.

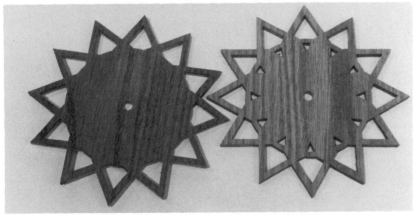

Illus. 360. Dark and natural Watco oils work well on oak and other fine hardwoods.

fretwork looks best with a natural wood look.

Good-quality hardwoods take stains and pigmented oil finishes much more uniformly than softwoods. (See Illus. 360.) One finish that is attractive and very easy to use is Watco Danish Oil. (See Illus. 361 and 362.) This thin, penetrating product comes either natural or pigmented in a variety of wood tone colors. It is not glossy, and gives a very rich, flat finish. It is probably one of the easiest types of finishes to use.

Watco Danish Oil is a blend of resins that penetrates deeply into the wood and, once fully cured (about 30 days), actually hardens the surface of the wood. Curing occurs through polymerization, which is a chemical reaction with the natural substances within the wood itself.

To use Watco Danish Oil, simply apply it to all surfaces with a rag or foam brush for approximately ½ hour or until the wood does not absorb any more finish. (See Illus. 363.) Wipe off all the excess finish with a dry rag.

The best finishes to use on softwoods are probably natural, non-pigmented finishes. Natural Watco Danish Oil sometimes looks good on pine; at other times, it does not. The

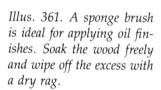

Illus. 361. A sponge brush is ideal for applying oil finishes. Soak the wood freely and wipe off the excess with a dry rag.

Illus. 362. Make sure that excess oil finishes are not left on surfaces or have dripped into tiny crevices. The oil must penetrate into the wood or be wiped off the surface; otherwise, it will become sticky. This project has a backer board, and should be turned over so that excess oils will drip out of the many small pockets; then wipe it as dry as possible with an absorbent rag.

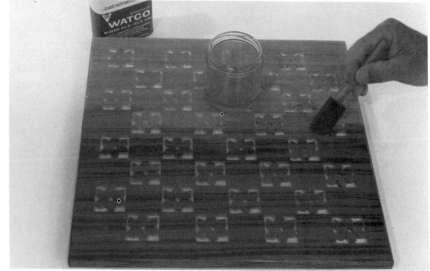

Illus. 363. Some typical finishing tools include foamtype and fine brushes. The flexible palette knife shown is useful for lifting patterns, levelling fillers, and for numerous other jobs.

quality of the wood may play a factor here; if it is pitch-loaded, not many finishes of any kind will produce good results. Film-forming finishes such as varnish or lacquer may be the best choices in certain situations when softwoods are used.

Clear Deft® is another useful finish. (See Illus. 364.) Deft® is a film-forming or surface finish that can be brushed on very easily. Some softwoods do absorb too much of this finish, and in such cases you may have to brush on several coats of it, and then sand it in between the coats.

Deft® dries very quickly. It is thin enough in consistency to enter narrow openings and thick enough to control sags or runs. (See Illus. 365.) However, when applying any brush-applied finish, watch the sags and runs carefully.

Watco Oil and Deft® are available locally from most hardware dealers, paint stores, woodcraft supply houses, and occasionally from discount department stores.

LINING TECHNIQUES

Boxes and other fretwork are lined to either conceal interiors by eliminating the "see-through" effect or to enhance the general look of the project. You can use spray adhesives for this type of work, but always test their suitabilities first.

Lining can be put on various parts of a project, like, for example, on the inside of a box, behind grills, or in back of fretted cabinet doors. Various lining or decorative backing materials that can be used include plastics, papers, fabrics, leather, tagboard, mirrors, and painted or natural wood. If you use the wrong material or color, you can completely ruin an attractive, fretwork project. On the other hand, a particular color can complement or accentuate the fretted cutting spectacularly.

Lining materials should be flat, and not wrinkled, and should lay well. Thin fabrics and leather may need a stiff supporting board on which you will stretch the material until it's taut, and then glue it. In some cases, the material can be pulled around and stapled on the back surface of the project, where its out of view. Sometimes the liner looks better if it is not placed tightly against the back surface of the fret, but is instead set away from the fret slightly at some appropriate distance.

As when selecting a finish, check or test the attractiveness of all liner material before incorporating it permanently into the project. You've invested too much work into your project to ruin it because you've chosen the wrong liner material.

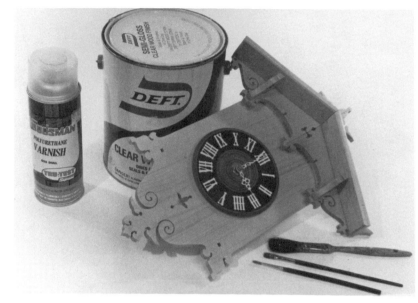

Illus. 364. This solid pine Bavarian-style clock looks great finished with clear, nonyellowing semigloss or satin finishes.

Illus. 365. Small brushes are helpful in small and narrow areas. When applying finishes with a brush, try to minimize the "sags" or "runs."

IX
PROJECTS WITH PATTERNS

The full-size project patterns and plans shown in this chapter are included to give you some immediate practical experience in fretwork. They are typical of other projects that can be made from the designs shown in *Scroll Saw Fretwork Patterns*, also published by Sterling Publishing Company.

In this chapter, you will also find a project plan for making a foot-powered scroll saw that closely resembles one used in the 1860s or 1870s. Also included is a plan contributed by Ray Lawler of The Tool Company for mak-

ing a very functional drilling device that incorporates a high-speed rotary tool with which you can quickly drill numerous saw gate holes. It is spring-loaded, so the power head drill always returns to the up position. This project was originally designed as a self-made accessory for the 24-inch scroll saw kit sold by Mr. Lawler's company. Fretworkers will find this device extremely useful for jobs in which many small holes have to be drilled quickly.

Illus. 366. One pattern makes all these shelves. Use ¼-inch-thick material.

Illus. 367. The pattern used to make the different shelves shown in Illus. 366.

Illus. 368. This optional alter-nate-shelf bracket design can be enlarged as desired.

Illus. 369 (above). The pattern for the shelf bracket. Make it from ¾-inch-thick stock. See pages 114–116 for more how-to information.

Illus. 370. A look at the shelf bracket.

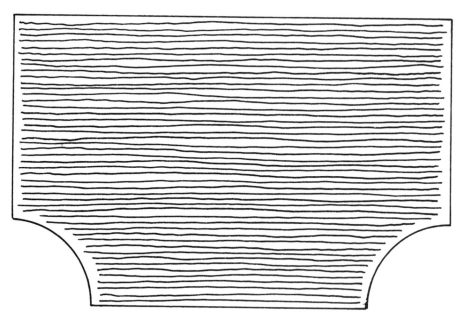

Illus. 371. A shelf project pattern. Use ¼-inch-thick material.

Illus. 372. The shelf pattern continued.

Illus. 373. A sign board end pattern. See Illus. 374 and 375 on the following page.

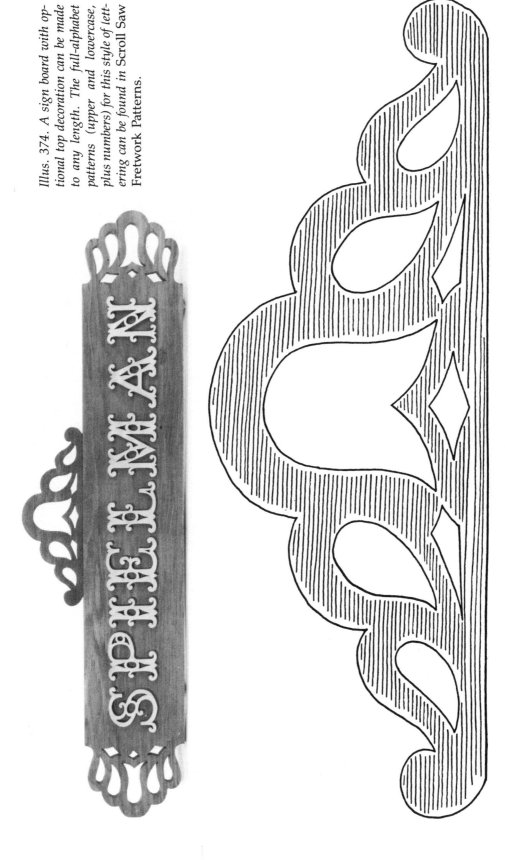

Illus. 374. A sign board with optional top decoration can be made to any length. The full-alphabet patterns (upper and lowercase, plus numbers) for this style of lettering can be found in Scroll Saw Fretwork Patterns.

Illus. 375. A pattern for the optional top decoration on the sign board.

Illus. 376. An Amish silhouette pattern.

Illus. 377. The Amish silhouette pattern continued.

Illus. 378. The wheelbarrow pattern for the project shown in Illus. 379. Cut all pieces from 3/16-inch-thick stock, and use a 1/4-inch dowel for a wheel axle.

Illus. 379. A wheelbarrow project.

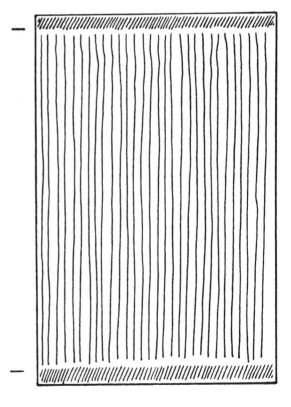

Illus. 380. The wheelbarrow pattern continued.

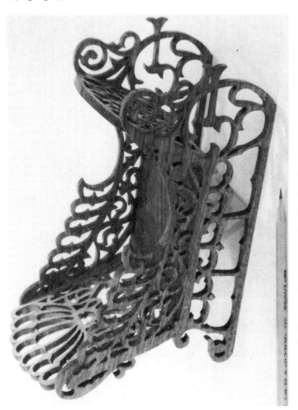

Illus. 381 (left). This ornate and deli-cate sleigh makes a perfect Christmas decoration. Saw both sides at the same time, one on top of the other.

Illus. 382. (below and top right.) The sleigh patterns. Use ⅛ or ¾₆-inch-thick material and cut a bottom to fit.

180

Illus. 383. A pattern for the wall clock shown in Illus. 387.

A   B

ROOF
(2 Pieces)

BOTTOM FILLER

BOTTOM

BACK

Illus. 384. The wall clock pattern continued.

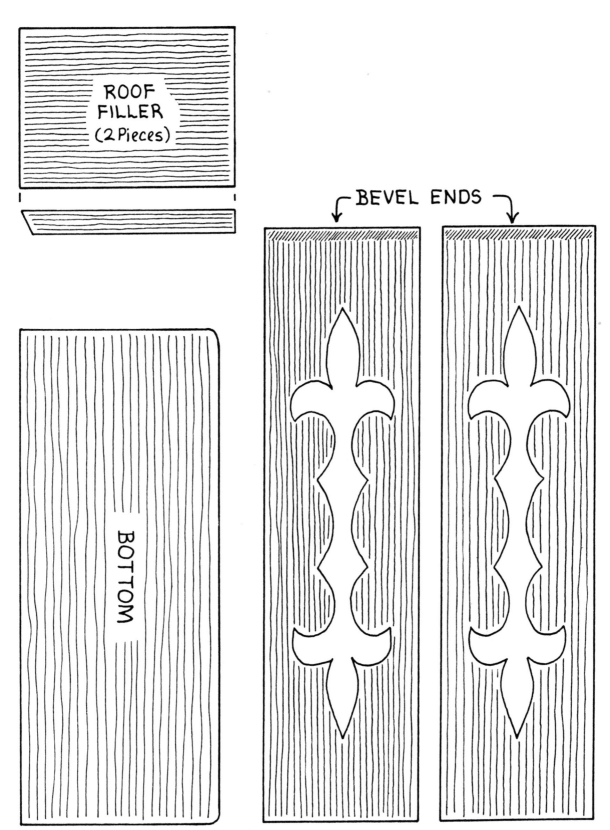

ROOF FILLER (2 Pieces)

BEVEL ENDS

BOTTOM

Illus. 385. The wall clock pattern continued.

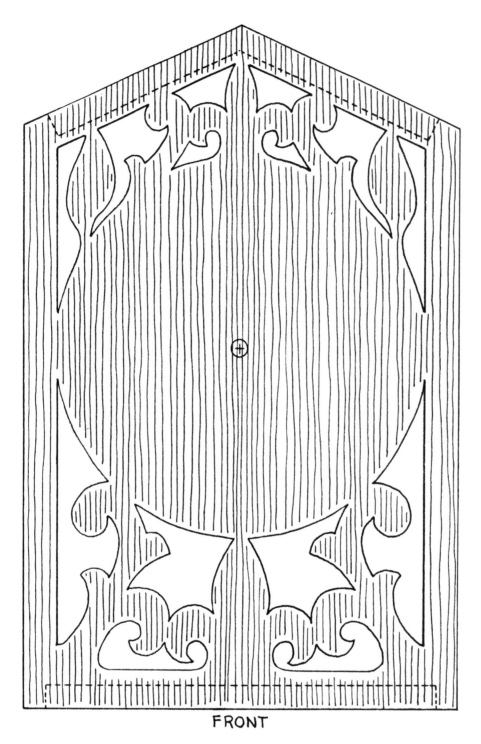

FRONT

Illus. 386. The wall clock pattern continued.

Illus. 387. This small wall clock, made of ¼-inch thick material, is a good project that involves basic assembly work. Refer to pages 157–162 for more how-to information. The 3¾-inch-diameter time ring and the clock movement are available from Reidle Products, Box 58, Yuba, Wisconsin 54634, and from Klockit, P.O. Box 629, Lake Geneva, Wisconsin 53147.

Illus. 388 (below left). This version of an 1870 foot-powered saw is a fun project to make and to use. The rope loop can be worked with heel or toe, whichever is easier. Illus. 389 (below right). This saw is designed to carry 7-inch-long pin-end coping saw blades with their pins removed. A V-board cutting table supports the work. Other larger table configurations would be a design improvement.

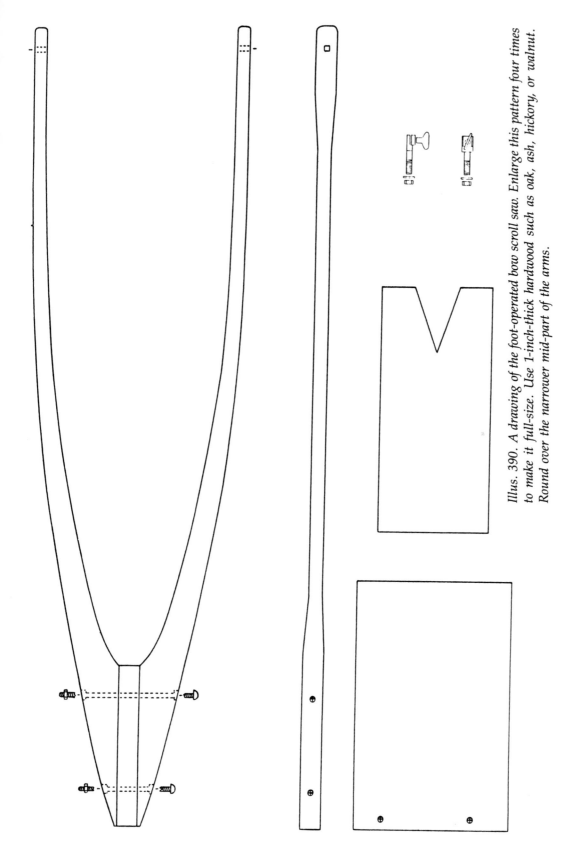

Illus. 390. A drawing of the foot-operated bow scroll saw. Enlarge this pattern four times to make it full-size. Use 1-inch-thick hardwood such as oak, ash, hickory, or walnut. Round over the narrower mid-part of the arms.

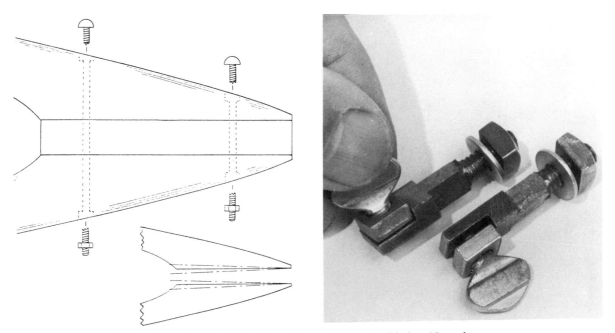

Illus. 391 (above left). A ³⁄₁₆-inch threaded rod can be used instead of bolts. Note the counterbored holes for the heads and nuts. The drawing at lower right shows how the heels of the arms can be modified to change blade size and/or blade tension by changing the base angle. Illus. 392 (above right). A close-up look at the homemade blade clamps.

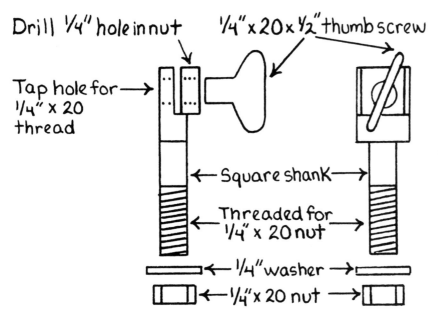

Drill ¼" hole in nut

¼" x 20 x ½" thumb screw

Tap hole for → ¼" x 20 thread

← Square shank →

Threaded for ← ¼" x 20 nut →

← ¼" washer →

← ¼" x 20 nut →

Illus. 393. Blade-holder details. Make two blade holders.

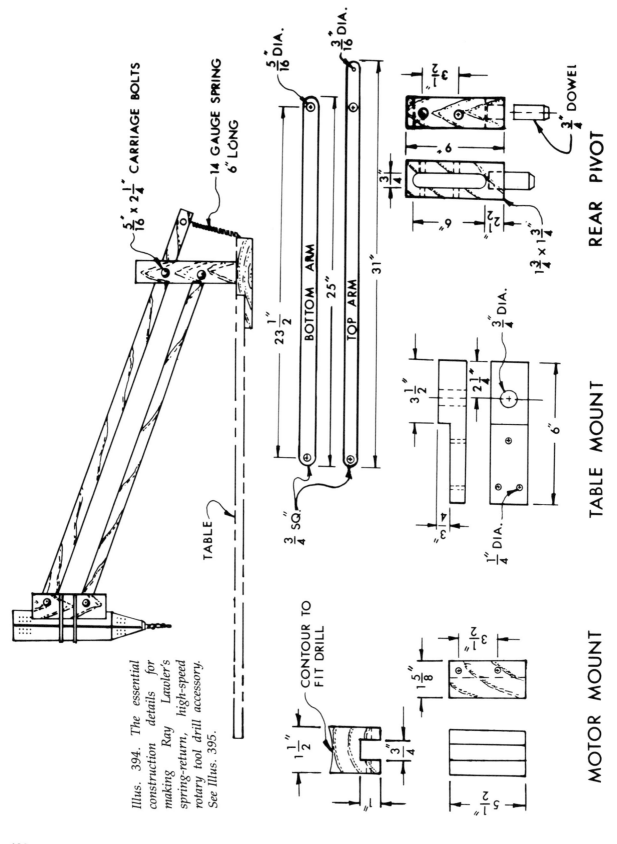

188

Illus. 394. The essential construction details for making Ray Lawler's spring-return, high-speed rotary tool drill accessory. See Illus. 395.

$\frac{5}{16}'' \times 2\frac{1}{4}''$ CARRIAGE BOLTS

14 GAUGE SPRING 6" LONG

TABLE

$\frac{5}{16}''$ DIA.

$\frac{3}{16}''$ DIA.

$23\frac{1}{2}''$

BOTTOM ARM

25"

TOP ARM

31"

$\frac{3}{4}$ SQ.

$3\frac{1}{2}''$

$\frac{3}{4}''$

6"

$1\frac{3}{4} \times 1\frac{3}{4}$

6"

$2\frac{1}{2}''$

$\frac{3}{4}''$ DOWEL

REAR PIVOT

$3\frac{1}{2}''$

$2\frac{1}{4}''$

$\frac{3}{4}$ DIA.

6"

$\frac{1}{4}''$ DIA.

$\frac{3}{4}''$

TABLE MOUNT

CONTOUR TO FIT DRILL

$1\frac{1}{2}''$

1"

$\frac{3}{4}''$

$1\frac{5}{8}''$

$3\frac{1}{2}''$

$5\frac{1}{2}''$

MOTOR MOUNT

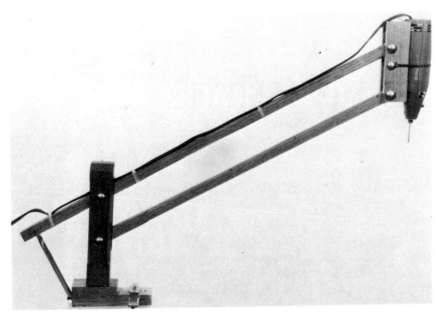

Illus. 395. Ray Lawler's spring-arm fretwork production drilling accessory incorporates a high-speed rotary tool such as a Craftsman or a Dremel Moto-Tool as the power unit. The rear (lower) spring automatically returns the power unit to the up position, as shown here. This device was originally designed as a do-it-yourself accessory for The Tool Company's 24-inch kit scroll saw.

Illus. 396 (above left). Soft wire clamps the power unit to a formed motor mounting block. Illus. 397 (right). The lower rear assembly. Note the 6-inch coil spring on the left.

189

X
GALLERY OF FRETWORK

This chapter contains illustrations of various pieces of fretwork. They are included here to inspire or motivate you and to illustrate the vast range of fretwork projects that were made by just a few individuals. The projects range in size from miniature wall accessories that are not much bigger than a dime to huge grandfather clocks measuring as high as 7 feet, 2 inches. Each of the craftsmen involved has his own preference concerning project styles and the materials and tools used. Some of the project designs shown are exclusively the creations of these craftsmen; other projects are from classic pattern designs—some dating back as far as 100 years or more.

Illus. 398 (above left). This Apostle Clock was made of old cigar-box wood in 1920 by James Reidle, Sr., who used a New Rogers foot-treadle saw. Reidle uses this scroll saw for all his fretwork, including the clocks illustrated in this chapter and an entire series of farm machinery models. Illus. 399 (above right). The Arsenal Clock, which measures 8 × 16 × 36 inches, was made of Philippine mahogany by James Reidle, Sr around 1947 with a foot-powered saw.

Illus. 401. A mid-section close-up of the bell tower on the Arsenal Clock.

Illus. 400 (left). A close-up of the bell tower on the Arsenal Clock.

Illus. 402. The base on the Arsenal Clock.

Illus. 403 (above left). The Chimes of Normandy Clock was made by James Reidle, Sr. out of butternut and measures 40 inches high. Illus. 404 (above right). This close-up of the bell tower reveals some interesting joint work on the fret pieces.

Illus. 405. A closer look at the two side towers.

Illus. 406. The mid-section of the Chimes of Normandy Clock. Note the "running trim" and the use of repeating designs.

Illus. 407. The clock base also has ornate fretwork.

Illus. 408 (left). This domed clock of butternut, made by James Reidle, Sr., is 50 inches high, 22 inches wide, and 12 inches deep. Illus. 409 (above). The bell tower. Note the small turnings, which were a popular feature in older fret projects.

Illus. 410. Narrow sections and cutouts attached on edge create the "dome" look.

Illus. 411. The mid-section and railings. Note the small doors, which have mini-hinges and knobs.

Illus. 412. The "portholes" are set over colored glass in each narrow panel. Note the arch at the left, which employs an overlay of the same material as the background and gives a carved, dimensional look.

Illus. 413. To avoid a "see through" look, a back lining of thin material is set about ½-inch behind the fret panels.

Illus. 414. The base features some shaped moulding around the bottom.

Illus. 415. The late Lawrence Boehner, of Orem, Utah, is shown here with his elaborately decorated fretsawn corner cabinet. Mr. Boehner, a professional fretsawer by occupation, began fretsawing at the age of seven. Incidentally, he cut all his projects using only a handheld fret saw.

Illus. 416. Animal cutouts by Lawrence Boehner.

Illus. 417 (above left). This flat deer shelf was made by Lawrence Boehner, who used a single pattern back to back. Illus. 418 (above right). This Swinging in-the-Lane flat wall shelf was also made by Lawrence Boehner.

Illus. 419. A spoon shelf designed by Lawrence Boehner.

Illus. 420 and 421. Silhouettes by Lawrence Boehner.

Illus. 422 and 423. Silhouettes by Lawrence Boehner.

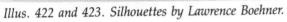

Illus. 424 and 425. More silhouettes by Lawrence Boehner.

Illus. 426. A display of miniatures by Kirk Ratajesak of Clinton, Wisconsin. (Note the dime under the sign for size comparisons.) Also known as the "fretworker," Kirk specializes in the production of fretsawn miniature furniture and scroll work for dollhouses. He will stack layers of thin material together and cut a number of pieces at one time on his Hegner Multi-Max saw. Kirk's products are often very close reproductions of actual Victorian pieces; some miniatures are made on a 1/12 scale reduction and smaller.

Illus. 427. Small mirrors by Kirk Ratajesak.

Illus. 428. Miniature photo frames also made by Rata- jesak.

Illus. 429 (above left). A full-size mirror shelf design by the "fretworker." Illus. 430 (above right). A square frame made by Kirk Ratajesak.

Illus. 431. This close-up shows how precisely Rata-jesak cuts his miniatures.

Illus. 432 (above left). The assembling of miniatures can present some problems. Illus. 433 (above right). This miniature wall clock by Kirk Ratajesak is very elaborately decorated.

Illus. 434. A miniature folding screen and other fretwork pieces that were precisely sawed by Kirk Ratajesak.

Illus. 435. More miniature pieces by Ratajesak.

Illus. 436. Miniatures made by Kirk Ratajesak.

Illus. 437 (below). Some of Ratajesak's pieces even have ornate fret overlays.

Illus. 438. Miniature tables by Kirk Ratajesak.

Illus. 439. Miniatures by Kirk Ratajesak.

Illus. 440. Chairs and cabinets in miniature by Kirk Ratajesak.

Illus. 441. This doll-house architectural trim was also made by Kirk Ratajesak.

Illus. 442. A stylized silhouette of the last supper, made by Kirk Ratajesak.

Illus. 443. Name signs and badges made by John Polhemus.

Illus. 444. Desk name signs.

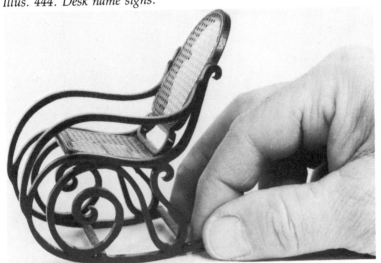

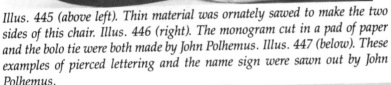

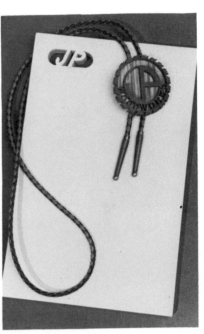

Illus. 445 (above left). Thin material was ornately sawed to make the two sides of this chair. Illus. 446 (right). The monogram cut in a pad of paper and the bolo tie were both made by John Polhemus. Illus. 447 (below). These examples of pierced lettering and the name sign were sawn out by John Polhemus.

Illus. 448. A personalized double heart-project makes a good gift item.

Illus. 449. A special desk sign that was made by John Polhemus.

Illus. 450. This door plaque for "Billy's room" was made by John Polhemus.

Illus. 451 (left). A scroll sawer's version of this family tree.
Illus. 452 (above). A family wall plaque cut out of mahogany by John Polhemus.

Illus. 453. Some very delicate sawing in solid mahogany by John Polhemus.

Illus. 454. The "family supper" sawn in mahogany by John Polhemus.

Illus. 455. This exceptional piece by John Polhemus not only requires delicate sawing, but patience and concentration as well.

Illus. 456. This fretsawn dragon, made light mahogany wood, stands out nicely against the framed backer of black velvet under glass. (The plan for the dragon is included in Scroll Saw Fretwork Patterns*).*

Illus. 457. Master fret-worker Carl Weckhorst, from Minnesota, produced all of the work shown in Illus. 458–480 and much more with the rigid-arm, 24-inch Delta jigsaw, shown here. Carl is a consistent blue-ribbon winner in local and state competitions.

Illus. 458 (above left). A partial view of Carl Weckhorst's fretsawn grandfather clock, which is 7 feet 2 inches tall, made entirely of ¼-inch-thick plywood, and has a total of 4,236 inside openings; it took Weckhorst nearly 400 hours to cut out these openings. Illus. 459 (above right). A basic wall shelf by Carl Weckhorst.

Illus. 460 (above left). A wall shelf with a bird overly by Carl Weckhorst. Illus. 461 (above right). This shelf by Carl Weckhorst can hang or freestand.

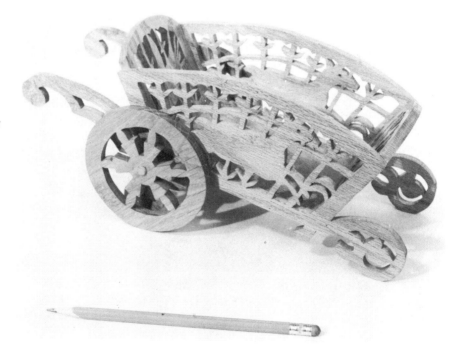

Illus. 462. A cart basket by Carl Weckhorst.

Illus. 463 (above left). A shelf by Weckhorst. Note the leaf veining, which is accomplished by sawing lines completely through the wood. Some veining canals be done with a veining tool. Illus. 464 (above right). A wall-hanging letter rack by Carl Weckhorst.

Illus. 465. A lidded basket by Carl Weckhorst.

Illus. 466 (left). A small fretsawn basket by Carl Weckhorst. Illus. 467 (above). A jewelry box by Carl Weckhorst.

Illus. 468 (above left) and Illus. 469 (above right). A fancy dresser mirror and a small freestanding cabinet, both by Carl Weckhorst.

214

Illus. 470. This flat cottage door silhouette by Carl Weckhorst seems almost three-dimensional.

Illus. 471 and 472. Bird cages by Carl Weckhorst.

Illus. 473 (above left). and Illus. 474 (above right). A tower clock and an English clock, both designed by Carl Weckhorst.

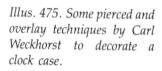

Illus. 475. Some pierced and overlay techniques by Carl Weckhorst to decorate a clock case.

216

Illus. 476 (above left). A scaled-down grandfather clock by Carl Weckhorst. Illus. 477 (above right). Some of Weckhorst's work involving the double overlay of fretwork.

Illus. 478. Note the fretwork and carving on this big project by Carl Weckhorst.

METRIC EQUIVALENCY CHART

MM—MILLIMETRES   CM—CENTIMETRES

INCHES TO MILLIMETRES AND CENTIMETRES

INCHES	MM	CM	INCHES	CM	INCHES	CM
⅛	3	0.3	9	22.9	30	76.2
¼	6	0.6	10	25.4	31	78.7
⅜	10	1.0	11	27.9	32	81.3
½	13	1.3	12	30.5	33	83.8
⅝	16	1.6	13	33.0	34	86.4
¾	19	1.9	14	35.6	35	88.9
⅞	22	2.2	15	38.1	36	91.4
1	25	2.5	16	40.6	37	94.0
1¼	32	3.2	17	43.2	38	96.5
1½	38	3.8	18	45.7	39	99.1
1¾	44	4.4	19	48.3	40	101.6
2	51	5.1	20	50.8	41	104.1
2½	64	6.4	21	53.3	42	106.7
3	76	7.6	22	55.9	43	109.2
3½	89	8.9	23	58.4	44	111.8
4	102	10.2	24	61.0	45	114.3
4½	114	11.4	25	63.5	46	116.8
5	127	12.7	26	66.0	47	119.4
6	152	15.2	27	68.6	48	121.9
7	178	17.8	28	71.1	49	124.5
8	203	20.3	29	73.7	50	127.0

YARDS TO METRES

YARDS	METRES	YARDS	METRES	YARDS	METRES	YARDS	METRES	YARDS	METRES
⅛	0.11	2⅛	1.94	4⅛	3.77	6⅛	5.60	8⅛	7.43
¼	0.23	2¼	2.06	4¼	3.89	6¼	5.72	8¼	7.54
⅜	0.34	2⅜	2.17	4⅜	4.00	6⅜	5.83	8⅜	7.66
½	0.46	2½	2.29	4½	4.11	6½	5.94	8½	7.77
⅝	0.57	2⅝	2.40	4⅝	4.23	6⅝	6.06	8⅝	7.89
¾	0.69	2¾	2.51	4¾	4.34	6¾	6.17	8¾	8.00
⅞	0.80	2⅞	2.63	4⅞	4.46	6⅞	6.29	8⅞	8.12
1	0.91	3	2.74	5	4.57	7	6.40	9	8.23
1⅛	1.03	3⅛	2.86	5⅛	4.69	7⅛	6.52	9⅛	8.34
1¼	1.14	3¼	2.97	5¼	4.80	7¼	6.63	9¼	8.46
1⅜	1.26	3⅜	3.09	5⅜	4.91	7⅜	6.74	9⅜	8.57
1½	1.37	3½	3.20	5½	5.03	7½	6.86	9½	8.69
1⅝	1.49	3⅝	3.31	5⅝	5.14	7⅝	6.97	9⅝	8.80
1¾	1.60	3¾	3.43	5¾	5.26	7¾	7.09	9¾	8.92
1⅞	1.71	3⅞	3.54	5⅞	5.37	7⅞	7.20	9⅞	9.03
2	1.83	4	3.66	6	5.49	8	7.32	10	9.14

ABOUT THE AUTHORS

Patrick Spielman's love of wood began when, as a child, he transformed fruit crates into toys. Now this prolific and innovative woodworker is respected worldwide as a teacher and author.

His most famous contribution to the woodworking field has been his perfection of a method to season green wood with polyethylene glycol 1000 (PEG). He went on to invent, manufacture, and distribute the PEG-Thermovat chemical seasoning system.

During his many years as shop instructor in Wisconsin, Spielman published manuals, teaching guides, and more than 24 popular books, including *Modern Wood Technology*, a college text. He also wrote six educational series on wood technology, tool use, processing techniques, design, and wood-product planning.

Author of the best-selling *Router Handbook* (over 600,000 copies sold), Spielman has served as editorial consultant to a professional magazine and as advisor and consultant to power tool manufacturers, and his products, techniques, and many books have been featured in numerous periodicals.

This pioneer of new ideas and inventor of countless jigs, fixtures, and designs used throughout the world is a unique combination of expert woodworker and brilliant teacher—all of which have endeared him to his many readers and to his publisher.

At Spielmans Wood Works in the woods of northern Door County, Wisconsin, he and his family create and sell some of the most durable and popular furniture products and designs available.

Coauthor James Reidle has been doing fancy woodwork along with general carpentry work all his life. He grew up watching his father create magnificent pieces of scroll-saw fretwork on treadle-type scroll saws. Years later, he wanted to recapture the best features of the early scroll saws his father used, so he developed one of his own, which is especially designed for fretwork and fine-detail scroll sawing. In addition, Reidle developed the first mail-order business in a number of years that is mainly devoted to fretwork patterns and supplies.

Should you wish to contact Patrick Spielman or James Reidle, please send your letters to Sterling Publishing Company.

CHARLES NURNBERG
STERLING PUBLISHING COMPANY

CURRENT BOOKS BY PATRICK SPIELMAN

Alphabets and Designs for Wood Signs. 50 alphabet patterns, plans for many decorative designs, the latest on hand carving, routing, cutouts, and sandblasting. Pricing data. Photo gallery (4 pages in color) of wood signs by professionals from across the U.S. Over 200 illustrations. 128 pages.

Carving Large Birds. Spielman and renowned woodcarver Bill Dehos show how to carve a fascinating array of large birds. All of the tools and basic techniques that are used are discussed in depth, and hundreds of photos, illustrations, and patterns are provided for carving graceful swans, majestic eagles, comical-looking penguins, a variety of owls, and scores of other birds. Oversized. 16 pages in full color. 192 pages.

Carving Wild Animals: Life-Size Wood Figures. Spielman and renowned woodcarver Bill Dehos show how to carve more than 20 magnificent creatures of the North American wild. A cougar, black bear, prairie dog, squirrel, raccoon, and fox are some of the life-size animals included. Step-by-step, photo-filled instructions and multiple-view patterns, plus tips on the use of tools, wood selection, finishing, and polishing help you bring each animal to life. Oversized. Over 300 photos; 16 pages in full color. 240 pages.

Gluing & Clamping. A thorough, up-to-date examination of one of the most critical steps in woodworking. Spielman explores the features of every type of glue—from traditional animal-hide glues to the newest epoxies—the clamps and tools needed, the bonding properties of different wood species, safety tips, and all techniques from edge-to-edge and end-to-end gluing to applying plastic laminates. Also included is a glossary of terms. Over 500 illustrations. 256 pages.

Making Country-Rustic Wood Projects. Hundreds of photos, patterns, and detailed scaled drawings reveal construction methods, woodworking techniques, and Spielman's professional secrets for making indoor and outdoor furniture in the distinctly attractive Country-Rustic style. Covered are all aspects of furniture making from choosing the best wood for the job to texturing smooth boards. Among the dozens of projects are mailboxes, cabinets, shelves, coffee tables, weather vanes, doors, panelling, plant stands and many other durable and economical pieces. 400 illustrations. 4 pages in full color. 164 pages.

Making Wood Decoys. A clear step-by-step approach to the basics of decoy carving. This book is abundantly illustrated with closeup photos for designing, selecting, and obtaining woods; tools; feather detailing; painting; and finishing of decorative and working decoys. Six different professional decoy artists are featured. Photo gallery (4 pages in full color) along with numerous detailed plans for various popular decoys. 160 pages.

Making Wood Signs. Designing, selecting woods and tools, and every process through finishing are clearly covered. Hand-carved, power-carved, routed, and sandblasted processes in small to huge signs are presented. Foolproof guides for professional letters and ornaments. Hundreds of photos (4 pages in full color). Lists sources for supplies and special tooling. 144 pages.

Realistic Decoys. Spielman and master carver Keith Bridenhagen reveal their successful techniques for carving, feather-texturing, painting, and finishing wood decoys. Details that you can't find elsewhere—anatomy, attitudes, markings, and the easy step-by-step approach to perfect delicate procedures—make this book invaluable. Includes listings for contests, shows, and sources of tools and supplies. 274 closeup photos. 28 in color. 224 pages.

Router Handbook. With nearly 600 illustrations of every conceivable bit, attachment, jig, and fixture, plus every possible operation, this definitive guide has revolutionized router applications. It begins with safety and maintenance tips, then forges ahead into all aspects of dovetailing, freehanding, advanced duplication, and more. Details for over 50 projects are included. 224 pages.

Router Jigs & Techniques. A practical encyclopedia of information, covering the latest equipment to use with your router, it describes all the newest of commercial routing machines, along with jigs, bits, and other aids and devices. The book not only provides invaluable tips on how to determine the router and bits best suited to your needs, but tells you how to get the most out of your equipment once it is bought. Over 800 photos and illustrations. 384 pages.

Scroll Saw Handbook. This companion volume to *Scroll Saw Pattern Book* covers the essentials of this versatile tool, including the basics (how scroll saws work, blades to use, etc.) and the advantages and disadvantages of the general types and specific brand-name models available on the market. All cutting techniques are detailed, including compound and bevel sawing, making inlays, reliefs, and recesses, cutting metals and other nonwoods, and marquetry. There's even a section on transferring patterns to wood! Over 500 illustrations. 256 pages.

Scroll Saw Fretwork Patterns. This companion book to *Scroll Saw Fretwork Techniques and Projects* features over 200 fabulous full-size fretwork patterns. These patterns include the most popular classic designs of the past, plus an array of imaginative contemporary ones. Choose from a variety of numbers, signs, brackets, animals, miniatures, and silhouettes, and many more. 256 pages.

Scroll Saw Pattern Book. This companion book to *Scroll Saw Handbook* contains over 450 workable patterns for making wall plaques, refrigerator magnets, candle holders, pegboards, jewelry, ornaments, shelves, brackets, picture frames, signboards, and many more projects. Beginners and experienced scroll saw users alike will find something to intrigue and challenge them. 256 pages.

Scroll Saw Puzzle Patterns. 80 full-size patterns for jigsaw puzzles, standup puzzles and inlay puzzles. With meticulous attention to detail, Patrick and Patricia Spielman provide instruction and step-by-step photos, along with tips on tools and wood selections, for making standup puzzles in the shape of dinosaurs, camels, hippopotamuses, alligators—even a family of elephants! Inlay puzzle patterns include basic shapes, numbers, an accurate piece-together map of the United States and a host of other colorful educational and enjoyable games for children. 8 pages of color. 256 pages.

Working Green Wood with PEG. Covers every process for making beautiful, inexpensive projects from green wood without cracking, splitting, or warping. Hundreds of clear photos and drawings show every step from obtaining the raw wood through shaping, treating, and finishing your PEG-treated projects. 175 unusual project ideas. Lists supply sources. 160 pages.

MAIL-ORDER FRETWORK PATTERNS

The plans or patterns for some of the projects illustrated at random throughout the book are either the copyrighted properties of others, or are just too large to fit into the space limitations of this book. Full-size patterns for many of the projects shown in this book are in our companion book, *Scroll Saw Fretwork Patterns*, by Sterling Publishing Co.

The following patterns, among many others, are available from Reidle Products, Box 58, Yuba, Wisconsin 54634.

Eiffel Tower (Color page A)	$ 8^{95}
Apostle Clock (page 190)	$14^{50}
Arsenal Clock (pages 190 and 191)	$14^{50}

Chimes of Normandy Clock (pages 192 and 193)	$14^{50}
Domed Clock (Color page D)	$14^{50}
Dinosaur (Illus. 321 on page 149, plus two more styles)	$ 4^{95}
Swiss Chalet Model	$ 9^{95}
Lord's Prayer (Color page H)	$12^{50}
Shipping for patterns	$1^{50} per order
*Full Fretmaster catalog	$ 1^{00}

*Provides full description and price list for more woodworking plans and patterns, Fretmaster scroll saws, blades, special plywoods, hardwares, clock kits, small wheels, and related hand tools.

Index

Now you'll never run out of ideas for making great projects with your scroll saw.

SCROLL SAW PATTERN BOOK

By Patrick & Patricia Spielman

• •

This treasure trove of patterns (just one of the Spielmans' books for scroll-saw owners) includes over 450 workable patterns—every one of them imaginative, inexpensive and original.

These unique patterns—for wall plaques, fine frames, shelves, lamps, signs, inlays, marquetry designs, puzzles and more—are not duplicated in any of the authors' other books, and you'll find a whole range of tips on changing sizes and flipping and cropping patterns, as well as on woodburning, stencilling and finishing every project.